FROM BREAKDOWN TO BREAKTHROUGH

SIMPLIFIED METHOD OF DEVELOPING MAINTENANCE MANAGEMENT SYSTEMS

UNMESHH KAASHIKAR

ISBN
Paperback 979-8-89744-978-1
Hardcase 979-8-89777-698-6

Dedicated to

To my parents for their love and support

To my wife, without whom this would not be possible

To my sister, for love, caring and friendship

And

To my sons, Siddhant & Vardhan, for their love and friendship.

CONTENTS

Acknowledgements — 7

Foreword — 9

Preface — 13

1. The Turning Point — 15
2. The Journey — 17
3. A New Dawn — 27
4. Life – Simply Organised — 37
5. Understanding The Inanimates — 60
6. The "Building" Material — 72
7. The Inquisitiveness — 86
8. The Kind Of Work, Understanding — 89
9. How Do We Do, What We Do — 101
10. Standard Maintenance Procedure — 106
11. The Man — 109
12. The Measurement — 124
13. The Life - Full Of Surprises — 138

Thoughts — 143

ACKNOWLEDGEMENTS

I sincerely thank the people because of who I could learn so much about the topic of this book. Mr. Ghanshyam Pant guided me in my formative years in the industry.

Mr. Jayakrishnan Nair allowed me to experiment with my work, make mistakes, and grow; Mr Jagannath V. explained and helped me understand human values in my work life; and many more helped me become a better person. I sincerely express my gratitude to all of them.

FOREWORD

We are witnessing a major change in maintenance management. It is transitioning from an equipment repair service to a business process focused on increasing equipment reliability and ensuring plant capacity. Practitioners are shifting from a reactive cost-center mentality to a proactive equipment management philosophy.

One common belief among leading organisations is that maintenance is a business process and that formal planning and scheduling are key to its success. Yet, there is a shortage of practical references on the subject. Most articles and conference papers emphasize their strategic importance, but they do not explore the practical details. The author has overcome this challenge with his NARRATIVE. There is now a ready reference to elevate the action-oriented maintenance practitioner to the level of understanding necessary to make it work.

I first met the author, Unmeshh Kaashikar, during my tenure with the PepsiCo Food division as head of engineering in 2001. Since then, I have accompanied him on his journey as he transformed from an excellent technocrat into a strategically profound individual and a mentor par excellence. He has a superb understanding of the practices that lead to maintenance excellence.

"FROM BREAK DOWN TO BREAK THROUGH" is a breakthrough addition to the body of knowledge on maintenance excellence and achieving it through a "4M" method in maintenance management, focusing on identifying and addressing issues related to Machine, Material, Method, and Manpower in that order.

The author employs candid conversation in his narrative to portray, develop, and instills a series of simple yet groundbreaking philosophies into deft matrices based on equipment classification focusing on safety, quality, and criticality. Interlinking interdependencies to break down the machine into the last possible stages for clarity of understanding. Integrating into an effective and powerful equipment BOM relating costs and procedures to the actual realisation of costs versus criticality and effective scheduling.

Methods of maintenance, including emergency, corrective, preventive, predictive, and CBM, ultimately reach a reliability-based maintenance structure encompassing equipment OEE.

The management of these elements involves people with the necessary skill levels to assimilate, interpret, and execute.

I began pondering this book, quite certain in my pre-assessment that it would be just another one in the crowd. Very soon, it excited me as I was able to relate various incidents and occurrences in my own realm of experience and how they could have been managed more powerfully, leading to meaningful and impactful conclusions.

The clarity and precision with which various key and critical thought processes are portrayed stand out.

A must-read for all those who have maintenance excellence in their blood, for a clear understanding of "just what is required" in their workplaces, and to create an indelible impression on how to transform business thought processes into a veritable reality.

A must-read for any aspiring maintenance technocrat in the early stages of their profession, as it will provide a clear and decisive roadmap for making their work practices sensible and logical by undertaking simple processes sequentially and effectively, as can be discerned from this book.

I would strongly recommend that the maintenance connoisseur peruse, imbibe, and execute the logical methods and approaches depicted in this book, thus achieving "excellence in maintenance management."

Jayakrishnan Nair

Chief of Engineering

PT Pacific Medan Industry

Hayel Saeed Anam Group

Medan, North Sumatera

Indonesia.

PREFACE

"We cannot solve the problems by being at the same level we occupied when we created them."

"Through books and reading, you can acquire knowledge that equals the experiences of seven lifetimes."

"It is foolishness to believe you can learn everything solely through your own experiences."

These quotes have impressed me a lot & it is my constant and consistent endeavour to understand and address the problems and concerns in that light.

I firmly believe that knowledge and wisdom are the only solutions to the world's problems. The more we share our experiences, the more we know, and we grow better.

With this in mind, I thought of writing down the methodology that I learnt and implemented during my work in the industry as an operations management person. I am sharing in this book are predominantly about Maintenance Management. My expertise, or you may call it my experience, has forced me to pick up this topic for my first book. But the methodology can be used in many functions to build systems and processes.

When I started my career in the late 90s, the industrial systems in India were not very well established. We were developing an economy, and most of the systems-based knowledge would be restricted to a few learned people. Every time, I used to hear examples of Japanese companies,

American companies and whatnot. It was rightly so because the roots of the industrial revolution were never in India.

The examples and the business consultants used to give us examples of other industries in developed economies. I used to wonder when a Japanese company would give examples of the Indian way of working. Ha! Ha!.

Sounds interesting, doesn't it?

Another reason for writing this book is to make a record of things that I learnt over a while. We appreciate Western sciences and doubt Indian scriptures because we, as Indians, are not very good at record keeping. We learn by "Saying & Hearing" more than by writing it down. Maybe this book would have some instances of my learnings which can help others & they can keep referring it back as and when they need.

Even though the topic of the book doesn't fall exactly under the lively topic, I have tried to keep it conversational for ease of understanding. You can read it as you read a novel and can highlight or underline the notes as you do for your study material.

Hope you will enjoy it.

Happy reading…

THE TURNING POINT

Whatever happens, happens for the good.

It was a hot summer day, and Sandesh, a rigger, was engaged in lifting & shifting a heavy vessel. This vessel was to be installed at a platform height of 11 meters. There were six of them, along with Sandesh. All had finished lunch and were back on the work site.

Before breaking out for lunch, all the chain-pully blocks, crowbars, slings, etc, were installed and ready for the work planned for the post-lunch session.

Once at the site, all of them started lifting the heavy vessel manually as well as via a chain-pulley arrangement.

Supervisors were all standing a few meters away from the actual work site, and intermittent instructions were crossing amongst them.

The vessel body top was up, and the bottom conical vertex was still on the ground. First, they could make the vessel upright, and then, after taking an absolute vertical position, the full vessel will be lifted. At least, that was the plan.

In India, temperatures in summer can and would go up to 45 to 47 degrees C, and these people work for last 10 straight days, 14 hours a day. Keeping up with the procedures & adhering to them can be challenging unless you have a very good, headed superior in charge. Rakesh was such of the kind. He went to lunch with his rigger and the workers' team and came back to the site along with them. That saves time. If he carried the aura of being supervisor, first his team would go for lunch and then he would go. In such cases, we lose a lot of time. And Rakesh knew it very well. Though he had only 6 years of experience in the industry as well as this field, he was ahead of his colleagues in handling the projects work or such kind of maintenance work.

Rakesh was level-headed, always loved to follow procedures and had a keen eye for details.

So the team gathered, and after filling up all the safety forms and explaining the procedures, the lifting of the vessel started. The vessel was lifted by around 4 feet from the ground and was now ready for the next vertical lift. The place was very congested and tight for multiple people's movement. The rest of the plant was still operating at its full strength.

At that moment, "boom", one of the chains from the lifting chain, gave away with sharp sound and vessel came down on floor. Imagine 4000 kg of mass falling on the floor.

Heart skipped a few beats for all people. The top of the vessel came crashing down, and people standing nearby ran for cover.

Within 10 seconds, everything was on the floor. Rakesh & Sandesh, who were clear off the area, first ran for cover and then, after 10 secs, were the first ones to look at the site for anyone who might have got hurt or any other running process plant equipment that got damaged.

One of the six members of the team had bruises, another one had a fractured leg & the pump motor of the running process plant was thrown out of place due to the vessel falling on it.

Immediately, damage control action was put in place; people were shifted to medical rooms, and the plant was forced shut for the next 12 hours.

THE JOURNEY

A new beginning

———◆◆◆———

Rakesh was sitting and waiting for his train at the railway station. The train was in the afternoon. Train came right time and he boarded and settled at his reserved seat. A lot of people were moving to and from in the passage till everyone got their seats and were settled. Rakesh had got the reservation in the Tatkal scheme. He got the side lower berth of the sleeper class. Sleeper class was the only one that he could afford at that time.

The train started and in few minutes, an aged person came and sat on the front seat. He had the side upper berth. He was looking curiously and helplessly towards the upper berth. In all practical cases, the aged people, when they get upper berths in railways, inevitably someone will exchange their berths and the aged person gets either lower berth, or at least middle berth. That's how things work in India when you are travelling in train. It's a unique experience.

The old man was probably looking for someone in and around who could exchange the berth and relieve him of climbing up. But he saw an easy solution as the lower berth there itself was with Rakesh.

The old man: Namaste ji, to which station are you travelling?

Rakesh: Last stop of the train.

The old man: That's good. I was wondering if we could exchange the berths. You see, at my age, people tend to occupy lower berths. That will be of great help. Can you do me this favour?

Rakesh: No.

Silence for 2 mins, no one expected such a quick, blunt and rude answer. The aged man looked at him and then spoke no more, but he was observant, and anyway, the need for change of berth would only arise at night time; there were few more hours before that would be needed. He kept calm.

As there was a grave silence between both of them, they tried not to look at each other and instead started looking out of the window. The summer time, hot air, hot train compartment, fans hardly of any help must have had the effect. None of them tried to reconcile. After an hour and a half, suddenly, Rakesh's phone rang. He was also taken aback. He picked up the call.

Rakesh: Hello

On the other side it was probably Rakesh's friend or colleague.

Other side: Hello, where are you?

Rakesh: In train, going back to my home.

Other Side: Why?

Rakesh: When they kicked me out of the job, why stay back and keep spending the money here? It's good to go back home & then think clearly about the next plan.

Other Side: You should have stayed back; we all could have put pressure on management to reverse the decision and take you back. After all, you have been loyal and a person of integrity for all these years with the company.

Rakesh: No, brother, there is nothing you can do. If management was really ready to understand the matter, they would not make decisions superficially. Secondly they needed someone on whom the blame can be put & there was lot of pressure to take action about the matter. I think that is the point. All management people and staff are like that only. The worst part is none of my managers were even ready to take my side and speak to higher management. Everybody has to save their skin. That is all they want.

Other side: So what are you planning now? You could have stayed with me for the time till you get another job or service. Why so hurry about leaving the place.

Rakesh: I could have stayed with you; I have no problem, but how long? There are a lot of things going on in my mind; why bother you unnecessarily? Staying there and listening to other people talk about the same topic time and again will only hurt me more. So thought that home is a better place to stay for some time and think clearly about what to do next. Surely, with a termination tag, I don't think it is going to be easy to get another job.

Even though Rakesh was trying to keep his voice low during the talk, but still to be heard on other side with trains noise, it was obvious that the talk would be heard by all nearby people, & the old man was no exception. Though he was pretending to be looking out of window, his ears were hearing all the conversation.

Rakesh: OK, brother, I will call you once I reach home; then we will talk. & thank you for calling.

The old man, still looking out of window, took a deep breath and exhaled in kind of despair. He understood the background of Rakesh's denial to exchange the berths. He didn't say a word.

This silence was maintained till the time when evening tea came up. Both of them ordered tea, and the tea seller filled one cup and gave it to the old man first. Age commands these etiquettes from others. The second cup was filled for Rakesh, and he took it. Rakesh wanted to take out his wallet to pay but was on the rear pocket. He found it difficult to hold the cup and do the search around at the same time.

The old man extended his empty hand and gestured to Rakesh that he could hold his cup for him.

Great non-verbal understanding; he did not resist & took his help. Paid for his tea, and thanked the old man. Both reverted to their original position of silence.

For the next two hrs, both were busy with their thoughts. After ordering dinner, each one again remained silent. Rakesh was occupied with his thoughts & the old man was not aware of the facts and wanted to leave Rakesh to his thoughts.

After dinner, everyone on the coach was getting ready and making their bed. Rakesh went up to the doors, took out his pack of cigarettes, took out one and lit it.

Slowly, the old man showed up near him.

The old man: The dinner was OK, wasn't it? But you didn't finish it. Too much in a hurry for a smoke. Uh!. I quit many years ago, but looking at you and smelling the smoke brings back my memories. How many more do you have?

Rakesh: Around 5 of them.

The old man: Can I get one? I will purchase a few for you tomorrow at any of the in-between stops.

Rakesh: Yeah, yeah – No problem, Sir. Please.

And he handed over one and lit it.

The old man took a deep drag, looked upwards & slowly exhaled the smoke. The experience was like out of the world, he did not have words, he only smiled and started laughing, looking at the cigarette. With his head still downwards, but looked at Rakesh by raising his eyes & laughed again.

This time, Rakesh reciprocated. Both knew what went along with them when the old man took a drag.

Rakesh: I am sorry for being rude in the afternoon. You can take my lower berth, and I can climb up. Something was going on in my head, and that reaction was totally unintentional and unintended.

The old man: Thank you, son, but I didn't find it rude. It's your reserved berth, and I cannot compel anyone to do away with it just because I am aged. I should have booked earlier.

Both looked at each other, nodded and enjoyed their cigarette.

The old man: You looked to be under some stress. Is there anything to do at home or at the company you work for?

Rakesh did not reply. Why talk to strangers about our issues?

The old man: "Before I retired, I used to work for a company. It was a mid-sized company. But as I was nearing my retirement, they started assuming that I was anyway getting retired, so why bother him with work. So, they slowly started giving me less work. & within one year, the talks were like, - "why to keep him, if there is no work for him".

It happens all the time. All managements are the same. I spent more than 35 years in this company. But I am lucky that my boss was good, and he always stood by my side. few years back, I retired".

Rakesh: All managements are the same; they only talk about "caring people", but at the end of the day, it's only business.

The old man: Did you have any fight with your company recently before you started your travel?

Rakesh: Yeah, kind of. But it was not fight. It was a sided discussion and decision.

The old man: What kind of decision?

Rakesh: Decision to fire me, what else? They all came together, decided to fire me and then, to defend the decision, started to make stories of how incompetent or reckless I am in my work. For the last 6 years, they didn't find me incompetent? Suddenly, overnight, I changed from a competent to an incompetent person. Uh!. All are the same.

The old man: Care to talk about it?

Rakesh: If I start talking, then the remaining 5 cigarettes will get over. Ha! Ha!.

The old man: No worries. If it happens, I will do some jugad to get more in sometime. No worries, go on.

Oldman's cig was out. Rakesh lit another one.

Took a deep drag, looked out of door. His eyes were moist of tears in it. The old man could clearly see from the side view. Rakesh collected himself, looked at the old man and smiled.

"Two weeks back, they fired me", said Rakesh in a composed manner. "there was an accident in the company, I was supervisor and it happened under my watch. And because it was under my watch, I was responsible for the accident. This is what their explanation has been".

"and what is it that you think?". Asked the oldman.

"I think it was correct"

"Then what is it that bothers you"? Asked the elderly fellow

"Don't know, when I look back, the responsibility thing seems ok but penal action doesn't seem justified, at least severity of it. They could have given warning letter, monetary penalisation etc could have been done, but firing was too extreme. That is what I think. As if I am the only one who was reason for the accident".

"Hmm," and with a slightly longer pause, the old man spoke.

"Did you intend to do the accident?"

"What stupid question is that?"

"Ok, did you do everything you could have done then to keep everyone safe?"

"Of course, that's my job, and I did that. I understood the work, its procedures, what is needed, how it will be done, etc"

"Was there anything you could have done better at that time?".

"I wish I could have checked the lifting tackles myself", – said Rakesh.

"But that's not possible every time and for all the items to be used, is it?" Asked the old man.

"Exactly. I cannot be everywhere, every time and doing everything on my own" Rakesh's response was quick.

"So, you did think of some improvement to be done in your way of working, isn't it? But this is post facto, I mean, it's after the thing has occurred; you figure it out. right?"

"This is learning". The old man patted Rakesh's shoulder. "The revised method of working can be debatable, but first thing is that you must take this as learning and do not beat yourself up".

"It's easy for you to say," claimed Rakesh.

"That's right, it's easy to say, & difficult to implement" -responded the old man.

Tell me, what kind of work do you do?"

Rakesh replied, "I am a maintenance engineer, mechanical engineer by education, and for almost 6 years, I am looking after maintenance of the plant."

"So you look after mechanical maintenance".

"NO, though I am a mechanical engineer, but I have to take care of mechanical, electrical, civil work, instrumentation and all."

"That must be quite taxing on you. I mean, managing the field of work, for which you have no background for it, isn't it?"

"Yeah, initially it was like that, but later I could understand that what is point in knowing only in one field, knowledge is knowledge, why to restrict myself if opportunity is there, so went along with flow of work and time & now it is OK. I am not saying I am an expert, but I don't fear of taking on any troubling situation".

"& in only 6 years, how can I or anyone become expert in all things. Expecting such a thing is foolishness in itself. This is where I have been asking for support from the company to train me in becoming a better technical and management person in the maintenance field so that I can do my job better. But no one gave an ear to it."

"Nevertheless, no point now," Rakesh quipped.

"You love your job?"

"yes"

"A maintenance job?" exclaimed the oldman.

"Yes, something wrong with it?"

"No, no, not at all, you are the first person who loves maintenance job. No one wants to get their hand dirty. It's a thankless job, with a whole lot of blame to be taken if things don't work. But no one appreciates the good work. So it was a surprise when you said you loved it" – exclaimed the old man.

"You are right, but see, as an engineer, I always wanted to be around machines, and I love it. Moreover, I have seen that the knowledge level that you get by being a maintenance engineer is huge, provided you have the urge and curiosity to learn. This cannot be attained by any other stream of work. I want to be an expert in maintenance. That's how I love it," said Rakesh.

He had light in his eyes when he was saying it; for a time being, he had forgotten the misery that it had brought to him at this moment. The oldman looked at him with a smile.

"What, don't smile, I am seriously telling you. I love it, else what will I gain by telling it to you. You are a stranger, why to unnecessary boast and fake thing to you?" Rakesh pushed his thoughts.

"Good, good, but I am not doubting but still can't digest that someone can take maintenance as career path. But it's nice."

"So what do you do in maintenance, just out of curiosity?"

Rakesh laughed." Babuji, don't tell me you don't know what maintenance is."

"Yes, I know something. I know something about industrial maintenance, but not as good as you, so I asked."

Rakesh-" Babuji, it's 11 pm now, & only 3 cigarettes are left; let's go and sleep; we will talk tomorrow. We anyway have 28 more hrs in train together before we reach our destination. Ha!Ha!.

You can take the lower berth, and I will climb up."

In the next 10 or 15 minutes, both were lying at the exchanged berth. The oldman went to sleep in no time, but Rakesh was awake.

"I was quite rude to this old man, I should have been careful. Anyway, I have already apologised. Do I mean what I said to him? About the love for maintenance field or I was just wanted to show-off?"

He went into thoughts, and the last 10 years were moving like a movie in his mind. Right from getting into engineering college, getting a campus job and then spending 6 years in this company doing lot of different things everyday & learning so much in such small amount of time.

A few months back, he had met his few college friends. During their discussions, it came out that only Rakesh was able to speak and talk about various machines and their performances with details; the rest of them were very superficial about what they were doing. Everyone had even complimented him for being a true engineer. They all appreciated that he had stuck to his profession somehow and how the rest of the others had wandered into different non-engineering fields even after doing engineering. He was feeling proud about this, and suddenly his thoughts came back to the recent accident. He could not sleep for the next hour or so.

A NEW DAWN

———◆◆◆———

He was woken up by the old man: "Come down, son, morning tea and breakfast would be here anytime, go get freshened up."

Under normal circumstances, Rakesh would have ignored the wake-up call and continued to sleep, but yesterday's rude behaviour with the old man stopped him & he gave attention. Probably wanted to make up for the unintended behaviour of the previous day.

He climbed down, got freshened up and again was about to go back to the gate for smoking. He asked the old man.

"Are you coming for a smoke? But now it's only 3 left."

"No, not now, but we will try that after our breakfast and tea. You can also wait till then." Said the old man.

"Yeah, that is also ok, let's have it after breakfast".

In another half an hour or so, the vendors came up with tea and breakfast. Though it cannot be compared to the home made thing but having tea, snacks and meals in Indian railways has its charm. The consistency of the taste (or lack thereof) is mind-blowing. Whether you go from north to south or east to west, the variety would differ, but you will not get any taste. Damn consistent in preparation.

They want you to eat healthily. Ha! Ha!.

It's digital in that sense, either you eat it or you don't, no midway in having the railway food.

As agreed, after breakfast and tea, both went near the doors to smoke. Now they had 3 cigarettes, one to each & only one remaining.

"Babuji, you will have to do some jugad for more cigarettes. Only one left. This will finish in another 2 hours. What will we do for the next 16 hrs?"

"I will do something, don't worry".

Both lit the cigarettes. "You were going to tell me about your job. So what do you do?"

"Hmm, you want to know or just kidding me?" asked Rakesh.

"No, no, I am serious, go on." Said the old man.

"You know that the manufacturing plant or company will have a lot of machinery, I mean all types of machinery. My job is to maintain them in working condition and improve their performance," said Rakesh.

"And how do you do it?, I mean, you would have some 50-odd machines, right? How do you maintain all of them? At the same time,? It's quite a task to do it, isn't it?" asked the old man.

"50?" smiled Rakesh,

"Small size to big size machines, all put together it would be around 1100 machines"

"1100? That's too much; how are you supposed to keep all these machines in proper health all the time? This is too much. And you still like the job?

"Do you get time to sleep or even go home?" asked the old man with surprise.

"When I started my career, I used to be in the factory for almost 17 hrs a day. You are right; at that time, I only went home to for sleep, Breakfast, lunch and dinner. Everything used to be in the factory itself. But over the period, as we put working systems in place, things start changing, and life slowly becomes normal. But it took 3 to 4 years to reach that point." Said Rakesh as he was taking up smoke and blowing it out.

With a sense of achievement.

"It must be a painful journey", said the Old man.

"Yeah, it was a rough journey, but not painful. We did many things in the last 4 years to make everyone's life easier that way. If the production or company is down due to machine issues, it's a hell to all of the employees, so it's better to keep it running."

"So now how many hours you have to spent at factory after you have done so much of work.?".

"Now it's 14 hrs, approx.," replied Rakesh.

"So from 17 hrs per day to 14 hrs per day in 4 years, is that an achievement?" asked the old man, while he blew the smoke.

Rakesh felt like stabbed in the chest. Turned and stared into the old man's eyes.

The old man understood and mumbled to rephrase the question.

But a simple question had hit the head already. Rakesh did not defend, "Not very great progress, but yes, improvement is there. A lot of efforts have gone to move from 17 hrs to 14 hrs."

"No doubt, yes, I am not denying the efforts, but for a person with calibre like yours, the person who loves his work, should take 4 years to achieve this, if at all you call this as your achievement." Said the old man.

Cigarettes were over & both moved back to their seating place; both now sat on the lower berth itself. The only change was that there was no dialogue for the next 15 minutes.

Rakesh was introspecting; he felt offended, and at the same time, he was looking for the genuine answer to his question. It is a simple question that makes one think about existence itself. He was very sure that the question was very much correct. But he has no point to defend himself, unless he puts blames to someone else for his non-performance.

"Non-performance?" what shit. How can this be non-performance? But yes, if doing the same work for 6 years is not allowing you to go back to your personal life & you still spend almost same amount of time doing it, it does mean that things have not improved. Isn't it the same as non-performance?

Rakesh was looking out of the window when the old man took out some roasted peanuts from his bag and gave him to eat.

Rakesh took it without trying to look at the old man. Chewed a few of the nuts and then looked at the old man and immediately looked away.

"Son, I did not ask to trouble you or question your competency about job. Don't feel bad about it. But if you keep other things the same and you are still working for around similar hours, you must think about what different thing you need to do so that you can also go back home on time. It may not be the case of punch in and punch out at the right time every day. But see from the point of view of 2 years down the line. Suppose you get married, of course you will, after 2 years. And even at that time, you work for 14 or 17 hrs, what will your partner think? She would say, Why did you marry her?

Okay, for the time being, forget what she would think, imagine your condition then. Right now, you are fighting only on one front; after marriage, you would be fighting on 2 fronts, and the hours of the day remain the same. You will have a 3rd front from your in-laws and parents & 4th one when you have child." The old man said calmly.

Rakesh's one fist was full of peanuts, and the other one was about to throw in one of the peanuts in his mouth when he stopped and looked at the old man.

"no need to be afraid of what I said, but think ahead of time and see what corrections you can do. That is all. Rest you have to tell me more details about what exactly do you do?" said old man.

At first, Rakesh had mixed emotions of annoyance and shock. In few seconds, he recovered and started telling his role and responsibilities and how he manages so many equipment and its maintenance, etc.

The old man was listening carefully and did not question anything while Rakesh was talking, sometimes exaggerating his achievements and all. The best part was that Rakesh was not thinking of the incident that happened in the company. He was not worried at all at that moment, and the old man was successful in manoeuvring his thoughts to something positive. He wanted him to think about something else instead of thinking about the incident at the company.

"In short, out of the 4 M's, you look after *only* the Machine part of it?" queried the old man.

"*Only*?"

"It's not *only*; all other M's are also required to look after this *only Machine* part of it, and now a days apart from the 4 M's its statutory compliance and impact on environment has also become big thing. How many years since you retired?" asked Rakesh.

"Almost like 12 years or so?".

"That's why you are not able to appreciate the changed world in the working of companies", Rakesh responded.

"Tell me, do you still practice TPM in your factory?" asked the old man.

"TPM, Ha!Ha! You mean Total Productive Maintenance, some say Total Productive Manufacturing, how does it matter? For us in our factory, it's called "Total Paint Management". Just before the audit or any visit, the areas are painted and repainted all the time. Gives a kind of new look, and that's it."

"Ok, that's very interesting, Total Paint Management, wow. But are you trained in its philosophy or methodology?"

"No, the company never took the time to explain this to us. Few managers were trained, and then they started telling us how to do the work. & that's how this paint thing started. If that is the TPM, then I would prefer learning something meaningful, rather than TPM." Said Rakesh.

"You are right," the old man said, "you can name any method; the true meaning is how you internalise it in a real sense. One may not be able to apply it every now & then or in every place, but knowing a correct concept always helps."

"Are you right-handed or left-handed?" asked the man.

Rakesh was taken aback by the question. But replied anyway.

"Right handed".

"Yes, so from tomorrow onwards, if I start calling you Bill Clinton, you will not be able to write with your left hand just because Bill was left-handed. You would remain the same, what you are. Just putting names to common sense and organised way of working is not going to change the basic concept at our subconscious levels. We must understand that these systems are meant to support or help. These are all guidelines, these would get tweaked as per the working of individual company's working culture and many other things." Explained the old man.

"Exactly. that is what I have been talking to my boss about also. See, they told me to start doing 5-S. The concept is good, in fact, very good. I know what steps to follow and how to implement the things, but if I forget the full form of the 3rd S, my boss says I have not been attentive during my training. Idiot! Those are Japanese words; why should I learn them? I mean, they want me to learn Japanese, then only I will be able to maintain equipment in India, what rubbish. As long as I understand what the concept is and how to implement it, how does it matter? What do I call that step in Japanese?" said Rakesh disgustingly.

The old man gave a good and hearty laugh, "Nice, you are right. So tell me how is it that you are not able to go back to home in time?"

Rakesh- "See, almost every day, as soon as I reach the factory, something or the other is broken down. I got a hold of the situation and start the work with my team. Once I am sure that the team can handle it, I start doing my work. I have to make daily reports, some analysis, material requirement requests, and different approvals & if I spend my time in the field more, then these things are delayed. So the work gets postponed, or I have to stay back and finish the work. On top of it, some work quality issues, meeting with bosses, meeting with cross-functional teams, an untrained or incompetent workforce, and sometimes material is not available, so we have to do some jugaad to keep the equipment running till the actual material comes. This is the same work done twice. So there are multiple fronts on which I have to face music throughout the day. And many a time, the cost control over the expenses itself becomes a painful thing. Everybody knows that to make the equipment deliver its optimal performance, there has to be actual cost input on it year on year, but they don't want to understand. Ultimately, the cost of all the production loss, the manhour loss in doing jugad and redoing it again, is not at all worthed if the decision makers had some brain. If not all, but failure on their part is one of the reasons that hardworking people at shopfloor level are getting squeezed on work as well as personal life."

The old man could sense that Rakesh was slowly reliving the emotional pressure.

"So, what do you do about it?" asked the old man, trying to push Rakesh from experiencing a problem frame to a solution frame.

"I don't know, & I don't need to think if it's now anyway, why bother?" said Rakesh in despair.

"That's right. Now, it's not needed for them, but it's for you and not for them. Secondly, we have all the time in the world till we the train reaches destination. We can discuss, and if I can be of any help, then consider it as payoff against the cigarettes." Laughed the old man.

"Yeah, that can be thought of", agreed Rakesh ", but you need to replenish those cigarettes you promised last night. You have to do that."

"Yes, yes, I remember. I will get additional ones in some time".

"Babuji, have you worked on the shop floor anytime with equipment to help me better my situation? Not in this company, but anywhere I go, the situation will be the same, more or less. Unless the company has good leadership and can retain them." Laughed Rakesh.

"You see, when we work in an organisation, it's evident that not everything can be done by a single person, no matter how experienced the person is. That is why, precisely, people talk about building systems so that the load is distributed, and at the same time, competent people are doing the work they are competent in. At least, that is what my understanding has been; correct me if I am wrong in my understanding," said the old man.

"Babuji, this is correct, but this is your expectation of the system. It is far away from what reality is. The gap between the system working and actual working is huge. I don't know which company you worked for, in our company its very much and huge gap." Replied Rakesh.

"Yes, and because there is a gap, we all have our jobs, right?". It was like the old man replied almost immediately. "If all systems were in place and perfect, we would not need so many people, so you can say that your job exists because of systemic inefficiencies in the company. Of course, the extent and severity of inefficiencies are different in different companies, right?"

Rakesh looked up at the old man with a little smile, as if the old man was questioning the existence of the "job position."

"In other words, we employees ourselves keep the inefficiencies live, to keep our jobs going?" Playfully asked Rakesh.

"Maybe", came a stern reply.

"Smart people do it all the time, but most of the normal people are trapped, and they don't understand that they are trapped." The old man tried to explain. If you keep doing the same thing for a long time, you will get used to it. Then it becomes your so-called "comfort zone", and then a time will come when you will start defending the position of "comfort zone" no matter how good the change may be. You will not accept it. It happens with most people, you are not the only one.

Otherwise, tell me one good reason for you to stay in the same operating condition for more than 6 years & then you defend that your work hours have improved from 17 to 14 hours a day.

Grave silence; the last sentence had been delivered with a slightly high pitch and commanding voice.

Rakesh was taken aback, not because of the slightly raised voice but the fact that whatever the old man said was true.

"I am getting brainwashed", thought Rakesh. Who is he to lecture me? His head was down, but he had a frown on his forehead. But at the same time, he was sure that whatever the old man was saying was the truth. Had it not been the age of the man who said such bitter truth, I would have abused him badly, he thought. His face was stiff & he looked up.

"Don't need to get agitated, this is the truth, isn't it? Or give me any other explanation for your condition," the old man started to talk as he looked at Rakesh's face.

"Ok, that means it's all my fault", quipped Rakesh.

"Yes". Said the old man, and looked out of the window. He could sense that Rakesh was still tense, stiff and restless.

"See, son, it's not about the word 'fault. First, it is the acceptance that something is not correct. The next level is to seek about how to correct things. At this stage, internally, you know that there is a problem, you might have tried a lot of ways to correct it, and it is not corrected. So, till now you have not got the solution to problem. But not getting a solution doesn't mean that the problem is not there."

"Ok Babuji, you tell me what to do, you got so much experience, I don't know in what, but the way you are telling me things, I can guess you can find a solution for my problem", expressed Rakesh in a tone that was not for seeking the answers but to challenge the old man. Rakesh wanted to use a different word instead of "Babuji" but still maintained the course.

LIFE – SIMPLY ORGANISED

Simplicity is the solution to all problems; the problem is to remain simple.

"Great, so let us talk for some time about your concerns, and anyway when we started with 4M's. Let us cover in that manner itself. We will uncover something new and learn few things while exchanging our thoughts", the old man said happily.

"You have 4 M's – Man, Machine, Method & Material and the latest you said is compliances and environmental compliances, etc."

"For simplicity's sake, let us keep ourselves with 4 M's only. We will see what these statutory and environmental compliances mean at a slightly later stage. You rightly said that I am not fully in tune with present progress on this subject, so let's take it up after some time," said the old man.

"OK, that is fine with me," Rakesh said.

"Out of 4 M's, which one is the most important one for you to work to be on time?" Asked the old man.

"All are important; every M is needed, or else how do I do my work?" replied Rakesh.

"That's right, but which is the MOST IMPORTANT one?"

"Without any one of them, I cannot do my job, so all are important," Rakesh said again.

"I know, but which one is the MOST IMPORTANT one? Making ONE of them the most important doesn't make others

Zero. It is just that to start building systems, we must start with one end of the thread. So I am just trying to get the most important thread to start with it", explained the Old man.

But Rakesh was still confused and agitated. The old man asked him to pull out a paper and write all the 4 M's like

1. Man

2. Machine

3. Method

4. Material

Then immediately, Rakesh said, "It is the machine that is important because rest of the 3 are going to work on it".

"Great, let's focus on Machine First", said the man happily.

"Do you have a complete list of machines or equipment that you have to maintain? Or list of equipment, directly or indirectly, you are responsible for maintenance?"

"Babuji, I start getting feeling that you have worked in factory shopfloor, right?".

"Why do you say so"?

"You are pushing me to do the things, and you seem to know about systems".

"Son, keep in mind one thing. For building a SYSTEM of work, you need not be an expert or experienced in that particular field, but asking the right questions and seeking logical answers can build an 80% accurate system. And then 10% of remaining is tweaked based on the experience and subject matter experts," said the old man.

"and remaining 10%"?.

"I don't know, for me, no system is 100%, there should be right balance of adherence to system and a big room for creativity. Growth is a function of creativity, and sustenance is a function of the system. Both are needed & not at expense of each other."

"We should be concerned with system setup first, then its adherence compliance. Don't push for 100% of anything, it only creates more issues. Seek for outcome that is keeping balance between all the resources." Replied the old man with a smile.

"interesting, but my management doesn't think that way". Said Rakesh.

"Don't worry, our priority is to get *you* back home in proper time & then we will see about the management part". Laughed the old man.

"Yes, yes, very correct"

"So, do you have a complete list of machines/equipment with you?"?.

"Yes, but it may not be complete. I can make it complete; not a big problem". Said Rakesh.

"Once you have the complete list, and you said you have almost like 1100 machines, small and big, all put together, right?. Which equipment are again MOST IMPORTANT?" Asked old man

"Most Important, now it has more than one, so many of them. But anything that stops production is considered a priority. So I guess the one that stops production will be around 150 nos." replied Rakesh.

"So do you mean to say that the firefighting equipment is less important and you would put them in second order of priority?"

"I didn't say that".

"But in your mind, you have second place for this equipment, right?. Ok, let me ask you one more thing. Is there any equipment that has chances where it can cause any accident to the operator? Like sharp knives, rotating blades, confined entry, etc?"

"Yes, few of them"

"So, if something happens there to any operator on those machines, still the production will keep going on?"

"No, no, it will be stopped immediately & all managers will rush there and if anything happens, we all will be bashed up" replied Rakesh.

"Great, that means it is not the production that is most important, it's something else., what is it?" asked the old man.

"Safety, of course".

"Good, so you know something about common sense." Laughed the old man.

"After you make the list, you cannot work on all the equipment all the time, therefore, you prioritise the activities on the equipment based on their 'Criticality' to the company or factory. Have you done it?" asked the old man.

"No, not till now. But I can do it. It can be done on safety and production base. Not that difficult". Said Rakesh.

The old man looked up and had the expression of slight despair. "So tell me, does your factory makes 100% quality product"?.

"No Babuji, tell me which company produces 100% quality product always, at least I have not seen it. Everyone says that they make 100% quality products, but it's not right."

"They are right; they make it a 100% quality product from the customer's perspective, always. But while making it or producing it, they may not have 100% quality output. The team in the factory works on it to make it 100% quality as promised to the customer. Therefore, I asked if there are times when the factory is not making 100% quality product FIRST TIME RIGHT. And there will be machines/equipment that help in creating the product FIRST TIME RIGHT (FTR). When these machines fail, do you still keep running the production?"?.

"Not at all. We have to take a stop of production. Do the corrective action and restart operations at the earliest. Till we restore production, we cannot leave factory."

"Then quality is also an important criteria for criticality, isn't it?" asked the man.

"Yeah, it should be, else what is point in producing substandard product?. And what does the FTR mean?"

"Sure, FIRST TIME RIGHT means the product that we get in first attempt with 100% pass quality inspection or qualifying criterion". We can talk more about it later." Replied the old man.

"Tell me, you have water supply at factory?".

"We have. What a question. Every factory will have it. It is the most basic need."

"ever happened that the water supply was not available to production operation or for people?"

"Yes, but rarely the supply stops. Because we have standby pump configurations. So, if one of them fails, the other one is started, and the supply remains uninterrupted. We repair the broken down pump and keep things operating". Explained Rakesh.

"Good, so for some items, you also have standby arrangements; that's nice. That means the items that have standby or have more than one support options, these are not critical at all, am I right?". Asked the old man.

"Yes, you can say that"

"But in any case, you must note it and then keep it for your knowledge that even the standby ones need maintenance. Hmm". The old man spoke while waving his hand and looking out of window, as though thinking and making up next question.

"What more can you think of when we talk about things that make any equipment critical?"?.

"Two more things I can think of, based on my experience. First is, if the maintenance takes a huge time, that equipment is always on every person's mind. As if they are scared of that equipment failure. Right from the operator, technician to staff, all of them. Second is the number of times the equipment fails. I remember, for certain machine uptime, even the factory manager used to take daily updates. It was so bad condition of the equipment". Replied Rakesh.

"So, do you mean the time taken to repair the equipment and the frequency of failure can be critical parameters to consider any equipment as critical?".

"yes"

"Do you run your factory all the 3 shifts, round the clock or is there any staggered working like. Some equipment or line works for only ONE or TWO shifts, or a line works for only 5 days a week, etc. Is there such arrangement in your production line and operations?"

"Hmm, there are few lines which run only 1 shift, some for 5 days a week but 2 shifts like that, but why?"

"See, what I am trying to see is, with over 1100 equipment in your factory, the number seems quite large. But to be effective, you should focus your time, money and resources on organising and prioritising the machines for maintenance. To get this idea, all these questions were asked. After understanding completely the answers to my questions, may be, you will find that you are not needed to be hyper focussed on every damn equipment, but may be only 50 or so. That will help you organise strategy for all the classification of equipment. The first and foremost thing is to get organised ourselves to help ourselves and others."

"Right, so what is your strategy to do this?"

"Son, I am not going to do anything for you. As I said, the right questions can help you unveil your strategy to handle your job or whatever."

"Okay Babuji, whatever you say." This was getting slightly interesting for Rakesh as he was finding it logical and felt connected to it.

"Tell me, whatever you have written till now." Asked the old man.

"No, nothing, except the 4 M's. I have not written anything; should I be writing something?"

"Your brain can process 5+/-2 pieces of information at any time. That's a fact. Hence, you should write down important things. I always recommend that people write down things. It helps in at least 2 ways. First – The new information is noted down and when all the senses are involved in writing – vision, hear and touch, it's difficult to forget. Secondly, even if you tend to forget, you can check back at any point in time later and use it as a reference. That way, over some time, you start getting organised in much better way," said the old man.

Rakesh rolled his eyes and then took out a diary that he was carrying in his backpack.

Started writing the points. For ascertaining the criticality of equipment/machine, the following things are needed.

1.   Production

2.   Safety

3.   Quality

4.   Time to repair

5.   Number of times the failure happens

6.   Standby availability

7.   Number of working hours

"That's very good. See, you remember it because it's still fresh in your mind. If I ask you tomorrow, I am sure one or two things will be missing from this list. But great, let's see if anything else we are missing that makes the equipment critical."

"There is no mention of the cost of repair, If it is a costly equipment or spares cost is very high then also management wants us to focus it. So it could be one criterion." Replied Rakesh.

"Are your manpower resources fully trained on all equipment repair? Do you find there is skill gap?" asked old man.

"No, how can everybody be trained in every equipment? That's practically not possible. Even if we *attend* the breakdown or preventive maintenance, everyone has a limitation that he cannot know everything, so in that way, there will always be a gap." Rakesh replied.

"That's right, so if I assume that for certain skill level work during breakdown or preventive maintenance, you need external support from experts, right?. Will that be or become your criterion for assessing any equipment for its criticality?"

"Not necessary, we have tie-ups with the service providers to attend this kind of issues, if they arise", replied Rakesh.

"Yes, that's correct, that's the way to handle the problem, but I am asking if this can become a parameter to assess the equipment on criticality. Suppose that the equipment is not critical on the rest of the parameters, but you cannot repair it by your people, and one day, this equipment breaks down. You called the external support, but he is not available for 2 days. Do you keep the equipment down for 2 days?. Look at it from that perspective. You have a contract agreement that is the method of handling the situation. That is good. But will that be a criterion for criticality assessment in first place?" Explained the old man.

"Hmm, possible, two things are different. Yes, we can take this as an assessment criterion".

"Good. Anything else, or any other parameter or criterion you think we should include as an assessment parameter?"

Rakesh added a point to the list and looked at it.

1. Production
2. Safety
3. Quality
4. Time to repair
5. Number of times the failure happens
6. Standby availability
7. Number of working hours
8. Skill required
9. Cost of the repair

"Wow, this is nice. These all points were there somewhere in the mind but putting it down and looking at it, gives a different feeling altogether." Exclaimed Rakesh happily.

"Yes, that's why I say, always write it down. So what next?".

"Nothing next. I have to smoke first. You have put a lot of pressure on my brain. It needs a good break. But I have only one with me, and you have not done any jugad to get more cigarettes for both of us."

"we can share it if it's ok with you. Friends always do that when they have little money left at month's end."

"No, no, it's ok. You can go ahead, have your smoke and come back. Till that time, let me speak to my family and chat with them for a while."

Somehow, after looking at the list of points, he was feeling happy, light weight in his body. No reason to be found but he was happy & that's why he craved for smoke.

Standing in the door of the train compartment, he lit the cigarette and enjoyed it. Waited there for some more time, looking at trees and the railway track speeding by. Many thoughts ran through his head. Felt the blast of air while peeping out of the door. Then, in a few minutes, he returned to his seat, feeling better and more energised.

"Nice smoke, h! It seems you enjoyed it; looking fresh". Said the old man.

"Yes Babuji, enjoyed it. So what next?" said Rakesh.

"You want to move ahead on this thing or just stop it here?" asked old man

"Na, na, we should look at it more. Anyway, there is at least an hour more before the lunch is delivered. So we can talk more about this. What to do next?"

"Yeah, the next step is to look at the list again, once. And set it right in the order of importance again."

"Importance again? Will it make any difference?" asked Rakesh.

"Yes, just do it". Told the old man.

"By the way, do you know how to bring out importance order in these items on the list?" By looking at Rakesh's face, he knew that he doesn't know how to do it, anyway, he asked him.

"Is there a way of doing that also?"

"Yes, very much. Here it is. Look at the list, take the first item, and ask the question, "Is this more important than the next item in the list?, If the answer is yes, then move to the next item and ask the same question. So you fix one item and journal the question through the rest of the items. This technique will help you compare each item with one another but in an order of importance."

"Let us do it for safety, and you will understand better, say, we fix safety in the list as item and ask this.

"Is Safety more important than quality?" If you answer yes, then safety remains above quality.

Then again, ask, is safety more important than production? If the answer is yes, then safety remains above "production". Go down this way and see how this list gets populated in order of importance. You will need some time to do this. So by the time lunch comes, you can do this."

Rakesh was amazed and had a series of queries, but instead of getting caught in the cycle of question and answer session, he decided to do it on his own and see what would happen.

After around 45 minutes, Rakesh reorganised his list in order of importance.

1. Safety
2. Quality
3. Number of working hours
4. Production
5. Number of times the failure happens
6. Time to repair
7. Standby availability
8. Skill required
9. Cost of the repair

Rakesh completed and showed this to the old man and at same time, expressed that the last 4 items, he was not sure if they have correct order. "In some way, the time to repair will depend on the skill set and also the cost of repair. Sometimes we do not keep high-value spares, and that may take additional time to repair, so I think the items 6,8 and 9 are interlinked and can be put it something as ONE item." Expressed Rakesh.

"Ok, what about others? Do you feel rest all are done and fine?" asked the old man.

"Yeah, the standby availability factor is also something to do about impact of failure, in a way that is leading to impact on production, and may not be relevant in first level of importance mapping. What do you think?" asked Rakesh.

"Ha! Ha! I am not at all helping you in this; I don't know this subject. Whatever you do, I take it as right. You can have a second look at it. But at same time, don't get bogged down by the whole thing, if it feels 80% right, let's move ahead." Said the old man.

"Sure, the list will be like this". He showed it to man the revised one.

1. Safety

2. Quality

3. Number of working hours

4. Production

5. Number of times the failure happens

6. Maintainability -Time to repair, Skill required & Cost of the repair

"Nice"

"The next step is to classify the equipment, all equipment, into A, B and C ranking.

The old man took the diary and pen from Rakesh and started writing something, it was in the form of a matrix / table. The table was something like.

Evaluation Element	S Safety & Environmental concerns	Q Quality output & Yield	W Number of Hrs/ Shifts working	D Impact on delivery / production	F Frequency of Interruptions	M Maintainability
A rank	Failure results in **serious** safety and environmental problem in surrounding area.	Failure would cause **defective product** to be produced or **seriously** affect yield	3 shifts working	Failure would shut down entire plant.	Frequent stops (every month or more)	Repair time 4-hrs or more AND / OR Cost of repair more than 100,000/-
B rank	Failure results in **some** safety and environmental problem in the surrounding area.	Failure would cause **quality variation** or affect yield **moderately.**	2 shifts working	Failure would shut down relevant or localised system only.	Occasional stops (once in 3 months)	Repair time 1-4-hr AND / OR Cost of repair between 10,000/- and 100,000/-
C rank	Failure will cause **minor** safety and environmental problem in the surrounding area.	Failure will affect neither quality nor yield.	Single Shift OR Intermittent operation only	Standby unit available/ more economical to wait for failure and then repair.	Hardly any stops (once a year)	Repair time less then 1 hr AND/ OR Cost of repair is less than 10,000/-

He made some simple lines for making a table and filled up the rows and columns.

"I have kept it simple; you have to ask the question as mentioned in the top rows of the column, and the answer that you get will define whether the ranking is in A, or B or C for particular equipment. Try filling out one of the two rows. That will help you understand better." Explained the old man.

Rakesh tried doing it by himself, and he had just finished one row when the caterer came and delivered the packed lunch. Both were hungry; they spread an old newspaper on the berth, opened the lunch box, and had some lunch. Both kept talking about how good or bad the lunch that is provided on railways is and a few other topics. The old man took good time, slowly eating the thing and looking around, then again taking a morsel. He took slightly more than half an hour to finish his lunch.

Rakesh had finished his lunch in 15 minutes and then spent time talking with the old man about his hometown, his growing-up years, etc.

When both finished their lunch, they washed their hands and came back to their seats.

Without speaking a word, both of them looked into each other's eyes.

"Don't look at me that way, you had told me that you will arrange more cigarettes. Now I have nothing with me, and after lunch, it is a must. I will have to go hunt around or beg it from someone. Do you have any real jugad, or you just said it for the sake of saying it?" Said Rakesh to the old man.

The old man did not say anything and just smiled. Rakesh went to another interconnected compartment to see if something could be arranged, at least a few numbers. Till the next big railway station comes and the train stops for more time, they will have to live with that. At that station they can buy some for next journey.

The old man had taken out an old book and was busy reading it when Rakesh came back happily and shared that he could arrange 3 more cigarettes. At least that will take care of evening time.

"I will not smoke now, you can go ahead and we can restart once you are back in seat" said the old man.

"Ha! Ha! I've already smoked with the other group, so no worries. I won't wait for you. Let's restart"

Rakesh filled a few more rows in the table, which was handwritten & showed it to the old man.

"Good, now our main task is to arrive at a consolidated rating for an equipment. For example, in the first row, there are different ratings under different criteria, but the equipment is the same. So how do we give an overall ranking to the equipment?" Said the old man.

"How?" asked Rakesh naively.

"Is there anything more important than the Safety of personnel or equipment?"

"No, not at all"

"So, if the for equipment the Safety rank is "A", then the overall rank of the equipment will directly become rank "A". now you can always debate, about it but my take is very clear, you ranked the equipment for safety as "A" that means there is something unsafe about the equipment and we must be vigilant about it. Secondly, it has high impact, or else you would have put it in "B" or "C". How you can make it safe is the next level of question, but as of now, if you rank it in "A", the full equipment becomes critical rank A equipment. Is this logic clear?" Asked the old man.

Rakesh thought for some time, looked at the ranking again by taking the diary back from the old man and studied it, and replied, "Yes, correct".

"Now we move to the next level, The next one is quality. Let's look at the quality parameter for the same equipment. If you have a quality rating of A in the box, that means any failure in this equipment will have a bigger impact on the output in terms of quality. Why should we have good quality product? Asked the old man.

"It is very simple, quality of the product creates a brand and the company will have brand value. If the quality of the product is not good we will lose our customers. In the long run, it is a very bad image for the brand. In this way it is not good for the business. The better the quality, the customers would increase, and the business will grow." Replied Rakesh confidently.

"That is right, very correct, so when the equipment is ranked A in safety, it directly becomes A-rank equipment. Similarly, you don't want the quality of the product to be at stake. The rank A in the quality box will make the overall equipment category has a. Very similar to ranking in safety aspect.

Now, let us assume that the equipment is not A in safety, but A in quality. Then what?"

"It will be ranked A, as you said earlier." Replied Rakesh. "Very good", said the old man happily." So you are grasping the things."

The old man continued, "Say, for example, if both of them are not in A rank, what would you look at next parameter or criterion?"

"The order of imprtance, I believe, that is what you asked me to spend so much time on before lunch, right?" hurried Rakesh with an air of annoyance about the question.

"Correct, correct, see I am getting old, don't remember things easily," and he laughed out.

"Try to figure out the simple common-sensical logic in this chart, fill one box and ask the question. In all situations, what would be your logical approach towards the criterion? The context is maintenance work, and you doing proper maintenance work to suit your time and resources is as simple as that. Try doing it and show me or tell me first and then you can write" said the old man

"For doing proper maintenance, material is needed and skilled people at the right time is needed. So we need to train people first and order and stock proper material; then only we can do maintenance," replied Rakesh.

"No, no, Son, stick to your chart. you are still only categorising the equipment to help you organise and prioritise the selection of machines for maintenance." Said the old man in little frustration.

"You should have the time to do the maintenance on the machine itself right, then only you can do something, right?" asked the old man.

"Okay, in that sense, I must look at how much the equipment runs daily. That means no shifts working, great, that's right. So, if I have one or two shifts running, it's not critical because I have one full shift available for me to do maintenance, or in case of breakdown, this shift can be used for production. Right, right. So simple. Nice." He was feeling proud that he could catch the intent of this and logically arrive at the proper outcome.

"I will do this part as well. If it's 3 shifts, I will put A, else B or C based on 2 shifts or 1 shift operations. Great. The next logical thing amongst the Production, that means what?"

"Here you can say Impact on production, instead of just production. Then it makes sense. Simple production has no meaning. Try that in this sense and your case its production, in other cases it can be any deliverables." Helped the old man.

Rakesh worked for some time with a questionnaire and filled the boxes accordingly, Slowly, it was getting very clear on the logic part of the overall ranking of the equipment. The complete table was getting ready, and he was bubbling from inside with a sense of joy. The old man could see Rakesh's face changing expression from tense to relaxed, and a gentle smile appeared on his face.

"Tell me once you are done", requested the old man.

In another 20 minutes, Rakesh was able to fill all the boxes and draw out the logical method to rank the equipment in an overall sense. He was trying to put an algorithm to what he did.

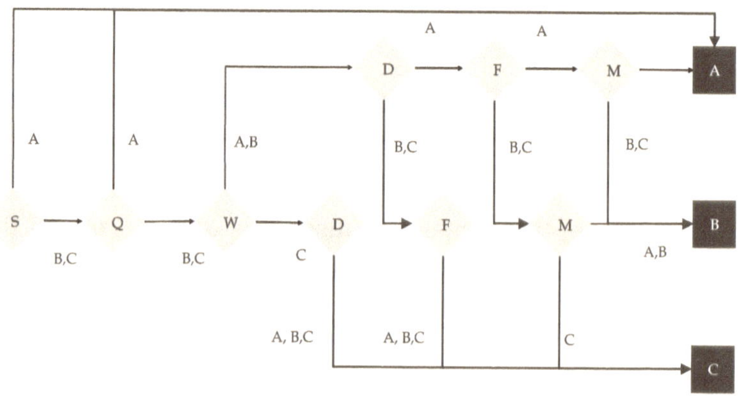

"You can do that later, "said the old man. You can draw it later for a better understanding. Now tell me, is 1100 of equipment such a big number to handle? What do you feel?" asked the old man

"Not at all, Babuji, if we organise things correctly. The action needed for each piece of equipment is based on their need, functioning and other parameters. Many such things can be cleared. We can stop overdoing and underdoing the activities and still be spending appropriate time at work."

Replied Rakesh, still looking at the chart and still making out a few more things.

"See, you have done a great job, This is the first step. You can have a different strategy to manage Rank A equipment, a different method for Rank B equipment and C rank it could be different. You have just been enlightened to the first step. We have not yet peeked into your actual daily work. Do you think this will help you in the way you work?" the old man looked at Rakesh's eyes. He could see the sense of relief and acknowledgement.

"Right then, let's move forward. make a 3 X 3 square box on a page." Ordered the old man.

And he wrote something in the boxes.

The matrix looked like the below.

Maintainability		Low	Medium	High
	High	1. MHE management		1. Inhouse team development 2. OEM support
	Medium		1. General Maintenance and Utility machines	
	Low	1. Outsource based on cost and time involved	1. Small tool management	1. Visit based AMC or 2. Skill specific driven contract
		Low	Medium	High
		Skill Level		

"Wow, this is fantastic," said Rakesh.

"Why?"

"With this, I can make out where should I put my energies into, which all items can I outsource, which I should keep directly under my control or monitoring, this can save cost and time both, plus I can make plan to train people only in specific and required areas only and do not keep training everyone in everything. Marvelous," Rakesh said happily.

"and more interestingly, this is only about the organising, selection and prioritising the number of equipment only, we have not yet gone into actual details of the maintenance of machines, and what you call as preventive, breakdown maintenance etc. There is more to come. Are you enjoying this?"

"Very much. No one told us about this. My boss is not from my stream of education, so whatever I tell him, he is not able to understand. How will he help me? Secondly, my seniors are not willing to tell me. But now I know that even they don't know things, that's why they are not telling me." Smiled Rakesh.

"Once we have organised this, what do we do next?" asked Rakesh.

"See, we are still on the topic of machine; that is M for machine out of 4 M's. Because you have already listed the equipment, why not get more information about these equipment at one place, in few sheets, or may be on excel sheet in computer now a days.?" Said the old man. "You can populate the equipment information data in a place. That will help you in many ways. It will tell you how much your factory load rating is, it will give you a count of equipment. It will give you how much of equipment are A and B or C rank equipment. In addition, all equipment has a standby facility or an alternate facility. Once the information is with you, the first thing you should do is to share it with at least 2 more people in your department. Explain to them the details to the last point."

"Few benefits of doing this are, one there is someone, in addition to you, who knows what data is available and, in your absence, can provide information to your boss or management for any required information. This will take off your load of being mentally always in the factory because bosses want new data now and then. It happens, right? For giving that data, you may have to travel down to the factory or open your laptop at home and then send emails, etc. If the person who is in a factory can do this, you are relieved of that mental load. Secondly, you are now preparing a second person to take up your work. That way, you are ready to move up the ladder, and he takes your place. The fact is unless you start doing your boss's work, 40% of his work, in terms of competency and capability, there are fewer chances that you would be promoted. And in many cases, even if promoted, you will still be doing the same old job role. What's the fun in that?. I will tell you what my guy in the factory used to keep it noted like" said the old man and again asked for his diary. He made some line there and noted a few things. Looks like the picture below.

Sr. No	Area	Function / Department	Equipment No.	Equipment Name (Description)	Make	Installed (Qty)	Active (Qty)	KW (Rating)	Total Installed (KW)	Total (Active) KW
1	Utility	Compressor Room	XXXX0000YY01	Air compressor	Atlas Copco	2	1	100	200	100
2	Utility		XXXX0000YY02	Water supply pump	Kirloskar	4	2	15	60	30
3	Plant and Machinery	Production	XXXX0000YY04	CNC machine	Makino	3	3	80	240	240
4	Plant and Machinery	Production	XXXX0000YY07	Conveyor system	Delta	5	5	5	25	25
5	Plant and Machinery	Production	XXXX0000YY08	Drying Kettle	KFR	2	2	10	20	20
				Total						

"Just go through this; this is only an example, not an exhaustive list. You can make your list based on these guidelines, you can add few more columns to make the information robust". Explained the old man.

"Phew!" Rakesh exclaimed. "We also have similar things, but not collated at one place. Putting it in one place and keeping it ready will help to make certain monthly report etc and will also help me organise things better. I can place the critical ranking in the same sheet in an additional column."

"That would be good and helpful to you", replied the old man.

"Great." Rakesh was still looking and flipping through the diary pages, somewhat not believing that this was happening to him.

Sensing that Rakesh was happy and interested, the old man continued, "These are all guidelines; you can make use of this and create your library. No one stops you. The results will be amazing, and the process you follow can be standardised. Can we progress further, if you still like it?"

"Yes, sure"

Meanwhile, the station was nearing, and people started to get up to stretch their bodies. Some wanted to get down, some just wanted to move around. And Rakesh wanted to look for cigarettes. "You sit, I will try to get hold of cigarette packet from vendor on the station platform", Said Rakesh and he left the seat.

UNDERSTANDING THE INANIMATES

Language of Machines

He got off the train. The train's scheduled halt was for 15 minutes. There is enough time to locate the vendor and get the packet. He came back with a packet of cigarettes and sighed in relief. "Finally, we have it. Nothing to worry till tomorrow morning." He showed the packet to the old man while he was talking.

After a few minutes, the train started, and people who boarded the train also were trying to settle down at their berth. After some time, "Yeah, let's look at what more you have in your store to teach me." Remarked Rakesh enthusiastically.

"Okay then, we looked at how you can organise yourselves with more information from data, right?. Because whatever I have told you, you had everything with you, so that is called data. The way I helped you to understand the same data by putting it in the matrix and grouping it helped you to draw some "information" out of it. That's the difference between data and information. Now onwards you have the information and you will utilise it to your benefit by working in more organised way. I hope you have got this?".

"Absolutely gurudev", Rakesh said teasingly.

"Till now, you have organised the whole lot of equipment spread around your factory in a more meaningful way in your mind and on paper. Now we will move to understand equipment as its independent entity." Continued the old man

"For you to become a good maintenance person, it is evident that along with the machine knowledge, you also need to have a good process knowledge. Only then can you understand the problems quicker and faster and also will be able to resolve the problems with appropriate solutions. I hope you agree with this"

"Very much"

"Therefore, as first step, you must understand the machine and how it works, as process part of it. To understand any machine, you must have basic information about the machine & then there is detailed information about the machine. You can have basic information like power rating, footprint of the machine, capacity, make, supplier, etc. You can have it as you like. A more detailed one will be like lubrication oil capacity, fuel capacity, rpm of the machine if it is rotating type, sensor details, controller or PLC details, etc. So, can you list out the items for any one of the machines for me so that I know that you have understood what I am trying to tell you?" Said the old man.

"Yes, absolutely, give me 5 minutes." Replied Rakesh, and he started writing down the list of items in his diary. After about 10 minutes, he had prepared a list. It had some 22 points. He showed it to the old man.

"It's a good start, I would like to reframe this into a format that you can easily remember." Then he asked to reshuffle some items and put them into a tabular form.

It looked like the picture below.

Sr.No	Particulars	Details/ Status	Technical Details
			EQUIPMENT INFORMATION SHEET
1	Name of Equipment		Power Supply
2	Function of equipment		Power rating of equipment
3	Capacity of equipment		Power supply conditions
4	Dimension of equipment		Earthing requirement
5	Length (mm)		Stabiliser requirement
6	Breadth (mm)		UPS requirement
7	Height (mm)		Compressed Air
8	Weight of equipment		Air pressure
9	Speed OR RPM (Max)		Class of air
10	General Arrangement Drawing of equipment		Flow rate requirement
11	Operation manual of equipment		
12	Maintenance manual		Water requirement (hot/normal/ chilled)
13	Must have Hydraulic circuit diagram		Pressure
14	Must have Electrical Circuit diagram		Flow rate
15	Must have Pneumatic Circuit diagram		Any specification of water quality - low TDS or DM water etc

		Details/ Status	
16	Must have Soft or Hard copy of PLC logic, if any		
17	Spare parts manual		Steam Requirement
18	Software version & license details with dates of expiry/renewal, if any		Steam pressure
19	Civil work related drawings - AS Built final drawings		Flow rate
20	Asset Code no of equipment for Maintenance Management		
21	Fixed Asset Register Code as per Finance Dept		Lubrication Oil requirement
			Full tank Capacity for lube oil type -1
	Additional Information		Full tank Capacity for lube oil type -2
	Supplier Details with contact of services & spares.		Full tank Capacity for lube oil type -3

"The whole idea is to capture the details as much as possible, but don't make it too cumbersome. If you see, I have added the water, steam, lubrication, compressed air, etc, in the same sheet. If any one of them is not applicable, write "not applicable" there. In that way, the data capture sheet remains standardised. No need to change it every time. Secondly, even if someone else looks at it, it's easy for him to understand and pick up the information that he wants. In addition to the above, you see supplier details, lube oil capacity details, type of oil, etc. All this information can help you to plan your consumable material. A lot of equipment will have similar consumables, which will help to optimise inventory and chances of using the wrong oil reduces. You don't have to keep everything in mind, but a one-pager will have it all if you want to refer to it at a later date." Explained the old man.

"Many things can come to light once we have things written down. There are a lot of insights from one page." Replied Rakesh with a sense of agreement to what the old man said.

"Here, I would like to go back to the equipment detail sheet for a minute. See in that sheet." He referred to the diary pages that had the equipment list. "If you look, there is an equipment number column. Here, you have to derive an equipment number system that can give you a lot of insights. For example, your number can tell you which factory you are talking about, its location, make, type, and category. These all can be clubbed into a numbering system. And don't look at it from a single factory or location point of view; define it for a multi-location, multi-factory kind of scenario at the beginning of the exercise itself. The unique numbers help to get next level of information for analysis at the end of the year about costs, breakdown patterns, time taken to repair etc. say e.g. first letter for equipment number can be P or even a number with 1, that means its factory 1, second number denotes location, 3rd number can be type, e.g. air compressor as 1, chiller as

2 etc, next could be make, next number could be rating, and last two digits can be serial number. That will help streamline the equipment number data. Now, if you look at the equipment information sheet, the same number can be put into this sheet. That can give you cross-referencing with the finance Asset code no. The equipment code can be numeric, alphanumeric or a mix of both, as it suits you and also the number of digits you can make out. Isn't it interesting?" smiled the old man when he stopped and looked at Rakesh.

Rakesh was looking at his face intently with a sly smile on his face. "Who are you actually and what was the work you did before you retired?. Don't lie; tell me the truth."

"Son, why would I lie to you?. I was in the finance department, and while working for our ERP system, I had to interact with all people. While doing that, our maintenance guy used to spend time with me, and that's how I came to know these things. He was a weird but intelligent person. Built good systems. That is why I can share all these things with you. You don't like it?"

"Liking? It's amazing. Wished that someone had told us when we started our career journey. It's wonderful." Replied Rakesh. "But you were to tell about the machine as an individual entity."

"Yes, will come to that. Tell me, when you go for maintenance of the equipment, how do you go about it?" asked the old man.

"We go near the machine, ask the operator about the problem he is facing, then we put our knowledge base about the machine and logic together and try to solve the problem. This is a very short way to describe what we do; it may take a huge amount of time. It depends on how complex or simple is the machine operation."

"Perfect, so you have to be knowledgeable about the machine working and functioning itself. And how do you study the machine or learn the machine to get more knowledge about it?"

"Normally, I ask my team or superiors to help me understand. That is quicker and easier".

"You are right, asking someone and learning it is quicker and easier. The downside of it is, if they have understood wrong, the wrong things get passed onto you & it will remain with you till you experience the things otherwise. Therefore, it is always good to learn from an OEM person for the first time, and if not possible, read the manuals first. Then, compare what you have read in the manual and what your colleagues teach you. I am not saying they are always wrong, but the chances of wrong interpretation remains there always." The old man

"What is your strategy to learning the new or old machine?"

"Strategy? What strategy? Nothing called strategy whenever the thing comes up. We go there, understand, learn and implement." Replied Rakesh, "Who has time to build strategy in learning method?" laughed out Rakesh.

"Yeah, it could be, but I will tell you methods to learn things quickly, at least in operations management."

"Let's say there is a machine, it has systems and functions. That makes a machine complete. That means, e.g. it will have a power system, hydraulic system, pneumatic system, drive system and many more, right?"

"Right."

"There are functions like conveying material is a function, moving the machine axes is a function, heating or cooling the product, mixing of the various ingredients or tool changing in CNC machine, inspecting the product, etc. System exists to Function."

"OK."

"The basic principle of learning complex systems is –

1. disintegrate into the smallest of independent systems. Till no further individual entity system can be broken down.

2. Learn this system and its functioning.

3. Interlink interdependencies

4. Integrate it back into the main system.

This is the simplest way of understanding complex operations. That is what scientists have been doing all along for so long & we study them."

"Wow, let me write it down, at least start the habit of writing from here and now, immediately," Rakesh said hurriedly as he turned his diary and started writing on a blank page.

"Coming back to learning machine or system of operation, we can have two ways to disintegrate and integrate,

1. We disintegrate the system first, study the function of it and then re-integrate/assimilate things back to understand complete machine functioning.

2. We disintegrate /separate the function first and understand the system. Then, we integrate our knowledge to create a complete map in our mind for a complete machine.

You can do any one them, which ever suits you. My maintenance person used to say that dividing the machine into functions first and then its systems helps to understand things faster. Its added advantage is that you can replicate this function-based knowledge to many other machines at the same time."

"Do you have any example you can elaborate on? I am still not clear about the difference," replied Rakesh.

"Yeah, give me the diary." The old man told and started scribbling in diary.

When the System is virtually divided, we study the function.

SR. No	SYSTEM	FUNCTION
1	Electrical	Stabiliser
		Control Cabinet
		Sensors
2	Hydraulic	Spindle
		Axes
		Automatic tool changer
3	Pneumatic	Spindle lubrication
		Safety Sensors
4	Mechanical	Axes drives
		Automatic tool changer drives
		Spindle orientation drive

When we virtually divide the Function first and then study the system.

SR. No	FUNCTION	SYSTEM
1	Spindle	Hydraulic
		Pneumatic
		Electrical
2	Axes	Electrical
		Drive
		Linear scale
3	Automatic Tool Changer	hydraulic
		Safety Sensors
4		Electrical

"There is a subtle difference; when you think and apply it, you will find it easier to grab the difference. But the other way round is also possible, it is up to you, which method suits you & ease of understanding. Take a minute and let me know it you have understood it." Said the old man.

Rakesh was smiling while reading both the cases, he was getting a glimpse of what the old man was trying to tell. He found it an amazing tool. It was a tool that could be used in various places of application. It was a learning method and can be applied to learn anything new. "Superb", he thought.

"Yes, I understood it, may not be completely, unless I use it once or twice in factory I will not have any questions at this moment." Said Rakesh.

"Good. The reason for explaining this at this point is that before you do any maintenance work, or for that matter, any work, you must understand what you are doing. For that, knowledge is a must. In your case, it was about learning a machine. And before we delve into further steps of building system, this is the first step. Now we can talk about the remaining 3 M's in our process." Explained the old man.

"Ha! Ha! I had forgotten where we started this. good that you brought this back on track." Rakesh replied jokingly.

"The remaining 3 M's are

1.   Man.

2.   Method.

3.   Material.

"Which one to choose to go about next?"

"We can go with this same sequence; how does it matter?" inquired Rakesh.

"Superficially, yeah, it doesn't matter, but if you want to retain something in your mind for a longer time and correctly, it is a must that you link it with some sequence."

"Just for the sake of discussion, you have 'Man, ' and you start creating a system around it. What do you want this man to do? Work on something, right? Where is that something? Secondly, you want him to work correctly and appropriately, so where is that methodology?. When you develop a system, you build a bigger canvas, but when it is to be implemented, it has to have solid physical means on which it has to be implemented. Are you getting me?" Asked the old man as he sensed that this was getting too much for Rakesh.

"e.g. suppose you say you are working on hydraulic system. What are you working on? You working on one or more components of the hydraulic system, without any exception. "System" is a virtual thing, created by the mind for ease of understanding, You "physically" work on the component always. Are you getting it now?"

"Now it is getting into my brain; before that, it was all going above my head. This example is good. You are right, we always work on some physical component to make system correct." Replied Rakesh happily as if it was an achievement to have understood what the old man was saying.

"That's good, now coming to choosing next M, if Man is there, but no Method what will he do? If he has a method, where does he apply the Method?. Common sense says it is the physical component that both Method and Man have to work on. Therefore, it's the physical component that you have to manage first. And this is nothing but the Material aspect of the maintenance. Am I making any sense?" Asked the old man.

"Yes, yes, of course, it's very useful, and I can understand you." Said Rakesh.

THE "BUILDING" MATERIAL

The Essentials

It was getting hotter during the evening; the sun was now directly facing their window seats, and the hot air was also making things uncomfortable for most of the passengers. There was still time, around an hour before the tea vendor would come and start serving hot tea. In India, for tea lovers, it doesn't matter if the environment is hot or cold. If it's time for tea, then tea must be there. Especially while traveling in train.

"I am having a dry mouth now, You can go through your notes again and see if you have any doubts. I will rest for some time. Or we can wait till tea time and then discuss this again. Is that OK?" Asked the old man.

"Yes, yes, no problem at all", replied Rakesh.

Rakesh got up and went about taking a stroll within the compartment. The old man went to freshen up.

After about 15 to 20 minutes, both came back to their seats. Smiled at each other.

"Get to see any pretty face?" laughed the old man while asking this to Rakesh.

Rakesh understood his laugh and said, "No, not on this side of the train. Went to 3 to 4 compartment but no luck, I will try the other side next time."

The tea vendor came in about 30 minutes. Both had tea. The old man wanted to pay for both of them, but Rakesh insisted that he would pay this time and that next time, the old man could pay. Both enjoyed the tea. Rakesh was waiting for the old man's nod to initiate the discussion further.

The old man disposed the teacup and said," Okay then, let's look at the material where we left it."

Rakesh opened the diary and refreshed the whole thing and stopped at the Material part of 4 M's.

"So are you convinced that after learning and organising the machine aspect, we must try to look at Material first and then Man & Method? I mean, if someone wants to manage with Man first, nothing wrong with it. It only makes sense and makes it complete if we start with Material first."

"Yes, you are right, we can start with Material." Replied Rakesh.

"What is this material? These are the actual components of the machine that you will work on during maintenance. Physical item that you need to work on to make the SYSTEM of the machine work. So identify the material requirements for machine first."

"It's like

Function → System → Assembly → Sub-Assembly → Component → Subcomponent."

Rakesh wrote it down.

"At some of the occasions, the subcomponent itself is the last component in the hierarchy where you perform the work, so nothing to worry. As I said, these are all guidelines. We can change or tweak them to suit us or our operations." Explained the old man.

He tried to give an example & asked Rakesh to write down this virtual breakup of the machine to subcomponent as he best understood it.

Rakesh recollected the talk and wrote back an example as below.

S.no	Machine	Assembly	Sub-Assembly	Component	Sub-component
1	Computerised Numeric Control machine	Automatic Tool Changer	Tool magazine (tool storage side)	Tool pockets	Tool lock
2					Tool lock spring
3				Driven Sprocket	Sprocket
					Drive chain
4					Sprocket bearing
5					Shaft
6				Hydraulic motor	End connectors
7					Motor seals
8					Hydraulic hoses
9				Positioning sensors	Proximity sensor
10					Sensor connector
11				Tool unlock cylinder	End connectors
12					Piston seals

"Looks correct. I don't understand what all these mean, but the flow seems to be correct. Do you think the Sub-component can be further broken down into individual parts?" asked the old man.

"Some of them, yes, for example, the drive chain, will further have parts which make it a complete chain when linked together. Do I have to go down to that detail?"

"See, we want to build a system that works for us and not create more problems for us. The guidance again will be like, if you are maintaining the chain by replacing its links or connecting pins then you should look at it, or if you normally replace it as a part in you management strategy, then stop at chain itself. The decision will be based on time to repair and cost incurred in an overall sense. We will discuss this later when we talk about maintenance planning. As of now, you can keep it till the drive chain level. No problem"

"With the sub-component level written down, what should be the next level of working? When you think of maintenance of these items, what do you need?"

"Yes, when doing work, how many quantity needed, what is replacement frequency, life of the item etc will be needed." Replied Rakesh.

"That's all required, but as I explained earlier, always organise things first. And organise it by order of importance. This gives you clarity in terms of the time and resources you spend on the list of items."

"So again, which one is more important amongst all these sub-components?"

"Yes. The most important item should be your focus during maintenance. And it is not that we neglect the rest of them, but priority and details are about the most importance ones."

"How do you find the sequence of importance for these items?" asked Rakesh.

"Eh! You forgot, that's why I asked you to revise and you went to look out for pretty faces," smiled the old man.

"Okay, okay, this is to be done similarly for machine criticality, right?" said Rakesh, explaining his annoyance over his remark.

"Correct."

"Don't you think it's impractical to do it for all complex equipment and all the list of equipment and then we derive maintenance management?. I mean, the management will kick me out if I say I am going to do all this and then do maintenance. It will take a huge amount of time on my part to complete this. I mean, it's a huge time for doing this for 1100 equipment." Cribbed Rakesh.

"It's a task, I agree, but not as big as you think it to be. It needs Logical sense, Common sense and Discipline to do this," replied the old man.

"This is where the equipment information sheet comes into play. I am not saying we don't have to do anything or that it is very simple, but when you are responsible for the upkeep of equipment in the factory, you will have to define and implement systems that will take care of things for you rather than you standing there at every place, every time. That was our first premise, right?. That was the problem we wanted to solve, right?

Now, let's check your fear with some data about it. Let's say you have 1100 nos.

Think about how many are strategically outsourced for maintenance.

Then, how many are C category machines which, by a strategy, are "run till breakdown" or "maintenance after breakdown"?

How many have standby machines?

Look at the data and derive how many unique machines are there where you have to do this exercise distinctively & exclusively?.

Secondly, the beauty of the process that we discussed is that once we virtually divided the machine into Function & System or vis-a-verse, the component level of the various machine will fall into almost similar kind of the components. E.g. you may have 20 machines where there is hydraulic system, but at component level they will all be similar to at least 60% of time, like, solenoid valve, pump, motor, level indicator, hoses etc. similarly for electrical also it will be one or more of relay, contactor, connector, sensor or PLC. Think about it.

In my opinion, you do the detailed map on one machine, and the same can be replicated to 50% of the rest of similar machines.

Still better, do this only for A-ranked equipment first, which will take of your 70% of your management load. I promise, things will start changing in a month. But whatever you do, look at the data that is built in the previous discussion and organise it. I bet you will find it a lot easier than you *feel* right now."

Rakesh started smiling and laughing.

"Why laugh? Not convinced yet"

"No, not that I am not convinced. If you look at the facts that you tell, it looks very simple, but doing it will take effort and time. But yes, what you say is logically absolutely correct." Replied Rakesh.

"ok, I can still go further. How many team members do you have in your team of maintenance, staff and technician level?"

"It's around 6 in staff level and may be 20 more at technician level. Why?"

"If I were in your place, that is a very good resource pool. You explain the whole thing as I explained to you to 6 of your staff people and divide the work amongst them. Let them work on six distinct 6 types of equipment. Share 02 equipment per person for A-ranked equipment. & then exchange the already worked out information that can be replicated to rest of the machines. I bet 60% to 70% of your work will be done. More people will get trained, exchange of information will happen, this will help to bring team together. They will all get knowledgeable, and you will have a common goal.

And for the technician level, give them B-ranked equipment. I mean, things are not going to be as easy as it's said, but improvement by 30% in the first month itself is a very good achievement. This is possible, provided you, as the owner of the process of maintenance, are organised first.

Rakesh was still laughing and smiling. Not because he was not convinced, but because he was finding it stupid that he had not thought like this before.

The old man continued, "Son, imagine the problem that you are into, the remaining 6 staff and 20 technicians are also facing, may be in smaller or bigger way. If you took some time to understand it, it is fair to think that even others will take time to understand this. Moreover, when things start falling in line, they will think of you as their saviour. They also want someone to come and teach them good things. Tell me, who wants to keep on doing rubbish things all their life?".

"Hmm, I agree. They look up to someone to solve their problems." Replied Rakesh.

"So we draw the criticality ranking on the subcomponent (spares or parts) as well. What next? "asked Rakesh.

"Then you do what you were telling me about quantity, make, type, etc. collect the data and specifications of the spares or subcomponent. Remember, the installed quantity can tell you how many to be replaced in one go, hence how many needed at one time when doing maintenance." Continued the old man.

"At this point, I would take a pause and suggest that it is prudent to collect as much data as possible about the spare part, keeping in mind the business aspect."

"What does 'business aspect mean?" asked Rakesh.

"See, your company is into a business for making profits, and until now, by your experience, you must have understood that maintenance of equipment, even though it is a must, it eats up the costs. You will have three costs,

1. Material cost in the form of spares replacement or repair.

2. The service cost of the work done, either by in house team or external experts, etc

3. The time value is when you cannot manufacture the product because you need the machine to be shut down. We may call it a necessary evil.

And for you to understand all 3 costs, you need to monitor them in some form. This is what is expected by your management as well from you. Because you are responsible for the department/function.

Therefore, now, keeping in mind that you will have to make some reports about business parameters at a later time, your information and data collection should happen while designing the system. For example, for item no. 2, that is service cost, the external service availed will have purchase order data from the system or payment data from finance. That will directly help you with service costs. But can it be broken down to equipment level?"

"I think so, some of the equipment possible, but not for all." Replied Rakesh.

"Why not all? & if it is to be done for all, what is needed?" asked the old man.

"The costs have to be booked against the equipment, & we don't have cross reference while booking the invoices." Said Rakesh.

"Right now, you don't have, but as you have coded unique numbers to all the equipment in your list of equipment, then it is very simple. The only thing is, when you go back, implement the system. Then it will be like clicking the computer and you get latest data about external service costs for individual equipment. See how the simple thing helps in multiple areas of impact?" smiled the old man.

"Then if we look at item no. 1, that is Material cost, for us it becomes spares cost, the moment you have spares linked to equipment and codified with unique logical number, something very similar to equipment coding. You can always get spares cost whenever needed. No need to dig out some data and then keep making it presentable now and then. The reporting time also drastically comes down for you.

In addition to that, the data is authentic, and you can use your time for doing analysis more often rather than spending time collecting the data. The more you are equipped with detailed, correct & timely responses to management queries, the more your boss and management have confidence in you and your way of working. This helps in many ways." Explained the old man.

"But it's not easy." Said Rakesh.

"No one said it's easy. I am just asking you to use your brain and think slightly ahead of the moment and accordingly create a format and system of data collection that will reduce your future repetitive tasks. It is not only about this system, but whenever you build any system. Think about its business impact and possibility of analytics needed for improving the matrices," replied the old man. "But don't overdo it; think not more than 3 to max 5 years down the line. Anything beyond that will be like collecting so much data that the data collection time itself is killing the probability of a useful outcome. Don't ever do that. It only creates delays and adds cost to the work. Try to maintain balance. Management is science as well as skill. You will learn it over some time."

"In this light, can you think more deeply about the spare part or sub-component and see what information you can gather by collecting data one time but using it multiple times at a later date? Take some time and think about it." Said the old man.

Rakesh looked at the broken down levels and started thinking about the spare parts quantity, "if I codify the spares that will help me make the query quickly while making monthly cost reports, if its coded then down the line I can get consumption pattern of the spare as well, this can be based on the issues against the material code from material stores." Rakesh was feeling happy about this. Saves him lot of time and brings in authenticity in whatever report he is making. " even now there are codified spares but the code doesn't help us in any way. Why do we still have to wait for material when there is a breakdown? That means stocking is not correct, inventory levels are not correct. There you go. I can define inventory levels also against each part based on consumption pattern." He kept on thinking for almost 20 to 30 minutes. The old man saw that he was feeling happy in whatever he was doing. So, I did not disturb or try to jump into a lecture.

After he was done, Rakesh shared the table with the old man.

S.no	Sub-component	Description of the Spare	Type of Spare	Install Qty	Criticality Ranking	Lead time for procurement	Imported/ Domestic	Unit Price
1	Tool lock		Mech		B		I	L
2	Tool lock spring				A		D	L
3	Sprocket				B	7 days	D	
4	Drive chain			5	C		D	
5	Sprocket bearing			2	B	15 days		M
6	Shaft				A	3 days		H
7	End connectors				C		D	
8	Motor seals				A		I	M
9	Hydraulic hoses				C		D	
10	Proximity sensor		Elec		C		I	
11	Sensor connector		Elec		C		I	H
12	End connectors		Elec		C			

"Superb, that like you have used your brain, ha! Ha!. Just kidding; don't mind. The inclusion of domestic and imported goods is very intuitive. It never clicked on me. And what is the last column H, M and L in unit price?" asked the old man.

"As I don't know the cost, I tried to put it as high, medium and low; once the cost gets captured, we can put the actual figures in there." Replied Rakesh.

The old man just looked up at Rakesh and smiled. "Now you are thinking. That's great"

"I know this is off track and not exactly in line with our flow of discussion, but when you stock these items and create inventory, you block the money in business. You will be knowing that, so do you have any plan or have you thought about how to keep it at optimal levels? This could be one of the reasons that the high-cost parts are not approved by management for purchase and stocking. And you feel that the spares are not available when needed. You can draw a strategy for stocking of spares," explained old man.

"As of now, we only either stock it or not stock it. What is the strategy in this? Is there any other dimension to it? Inquired Rakesh.

"Logic, logic, logic and organise, organise, organise and prioritise, prioritise, prioritise, if you want to make life simple and easier", shot back the old man. Took the diary from Rakesh and drew a table.

<table>
<tr><td rowspan="4">Cost of Material</td><td>High</td><td>Order as per requirement</td><td></td><td>High Material Cost & High critical – share with OEM or Comprehensive AMC mode</td></tr>
<tr><td>Medium</td><td>Mix of stock at factory, share with OEM, & Schedule Agreement mode</td><td>Mix of stock at factory, share with OEM, & Schedule Agreement mode</td><td></td></tr>
<tr><td>Low</td><td>Schedule agreement with Suppliers</td><td>Stock in Factory</td><td>Stock in Factory</td></tr>
<tr><td></td><td>Low</td><td>Medium</td><td>High</td></tr>
<tr><td></td><td colspan="3">Criticality of Material</td></tr>
</table>

"This can be a starting point to find out which material to stock, how to stock and where to stock, at whose cost can it be stocked. I mean, again, these are guidelines; you can make your matrix that suits you and helps you to make sound decisions about inventory management." Explained the old man.

"Babuji, this is very helpful. Very useful. If only my boss or management had taught me this earlier, I could have saved many hours of my life lying in the factory."

"Is the material part over or still more to be done?" asked Rakesh in a tired tone.

"You seem to be tired of this." Quipped the old man.

"Not tired of this learning, but tired of the material-related discussion. When will we move to next M's?"

"Once we finish the round of smoke, I need you to lend me one, I have not had it since morning." Said the old man.

They both went to the door of the compartment, both lit the cigarettes and enjoyed it thoroughly. Meanwhile, Rakesh checked with the Ticket checker if the train was running late or on time. Came to know that train was running late by 2 hrs and will try to cover the time delay in night time.

While still smoking, the old man said, "You must be aware of different types of maintenance, and you have to give me brief about them so that we can talk about it before we proceed to Method part of the system development."

"So we will not be moving to 'method' now? Still some time to talk about it?" asked Rakesh.

"Yes, obviously, unless you know "what to do", you cannot know "how to do". Replied the old man swiftly.

THE INQUISITIVENESS

Ask the right questions first.

Even after smoking, they stayed there for a few more minutes. Enjoyed the cool air blasts at the door as it was getting into evening time. The sun had not set, but the intensity had come.

Later, they came back to their seats after getting freshened up and settled.

"Now is time to align ourselves to 5 W -1 H, model of questions," said the old man.

"Wait, before we do that, there was the 3rd item on the cost part, which was like the time cost of the downtime or breakdown. What about it?" asked Rakesh.

"Good one, but I will get to that shortly when we do performance measurement. You will have to wait till then." Replied the old man.

"So, 5 W & 1 H, you are aware of that?" continued the old man.

"That I know", Rakesh darted back happily. "Ok, tell me how will you use it in our case and progress of system development?" asked the old man.

"Hmm! We can ask 5 W's and 1 H about the situation we have on material, I assume?"

"Try it and tell me what you came to know,, Replied the old man.

Rakesh thought for some time and understood that it was too early to jump to conclusions when he was not very clear about exactly where to use this questionnaire method and in what sequence. He kept quiet and looked at the old man, expressing that he needed to pitch in and explain.

"Right, there you go. Let's write the 5 W -1 H meaning, so write it in your diary.

1.   W – *What* – what do you want to do?

2.   W – *Who* will do : This we will discuss in detail when we talk about last M -Man.

3.   W – *Where* will it happen– Where do you want to do? What you wanted to do.

4.   W – *When* – When do you want to do.

5.   W – *Why*? Why do you want to do what you wanted to do?

6.   H – *How*- How do you want to do, what you wanted to do.

Out of these six questions, questions no. 2 and 6 will become part of the next remaining M's, i.e. Method and Man. So we take it at later stages.

Question no. 3, "Where" is the subcomponent where we want to do some maintenance work, so that is the answer to your question of "Where"

Question no 1, "what" is what exactly you want to do to "This" spare that is under discussion.

Question no 5: "Why" is the reason for doing it? So, maybe it is failing more often or failing for a longer time, etc. These are reasons for you to work on "this" spare under discussion.

Question no 4, "when", is a scale of time. So when do you do the work that you wanted to do, where you wanted to do.

The sequence of questions will then be like

1. Where

2. Why

3. What

4. When

Ask this sequence of questions to each sub-component of the machine, the answers will give you the map of your maintenance plan for that subcomponent. Do you want to try it out on any of the subcomponents that you wrote down in the previous example?. Just try it out on the drive chain and see if this pattern helps. Again, it's a guideline, so if you want to change the sequence, by all means, you are welcome to do that. Try it out once," remarked the old man.

Rakesh was amused by the way the things were presented to him; these things he already knew. I mean the meaning of those short forms, but the application of it was getting crystal clear now. Maybe he took it lightly when it was taught to him in the early years of his career. He took the example of the drive chain from an earlier text and got the answers.

1. Where – drive chain

2. Why? Because it fails more often or is already broken

3. What – tighten the chain or adjust or shorten the chain (based on actual condition)

4. When – Every 6 months (this is the frequency of doing work).

The moment he answered the "when", he was excited and shouted, "This is nothing but frequency of preventive maintenance, wow."

"See, you yourselves are giving all answers," said the old man.

THE KIND OF WORK, UNDERSTANDING

The devil lies in the details.

------◆◆※◆●------

Rakesh was still recovering from his joy and settling down. The old man asked,

"You said preventive maintenance. What types or kind of maintenance do you have, all put together?"

"It is like

1. Breakdown maintenance – very common, we all know.

2. Preventive maintenance – It is the work we do to prevent the breakdown from happening. It has two subdivisions.

    a. Time-based maintenance – it is done on set frequency, irrespective of the need of doing it based on condition.

    b. Condition-based maintenance- It is done during or after we assess the condition of the spares. If the condition calls for it, we do the work; else not.

    c. Overhaul – this is also time-based, but it's taken on a bigger scale. During the overhaul itself, we do both time-based and condition-based maintenance.

3. Corrective Maintenance – It is like correcting the thing that has gone bad. For example, the drive chain of a bicycle slips during the pedalling, and normally, we do tension adjustment. But sometimes, we have to shorten the drive chain by removing a link. And everything is ok. This is corrective maintenance.

4. Maintenance prevention – Some people say that it is the stage where there is no need for maintenance. I am not sure what that means.

This is what you were interested in, right?" said Rakesh.

"Correct, I got it now. Nicely explained. Tell me, which item, means, which type of maintenance will be used for which spare or sub-component, how do you arrive at that conclusion?" asked the old man.

"There is not a straightforward answer to this, but I will try to explain. It's more of common sense. For example, we all know by our experience or by the information given by OEM about the life of the equipment. And certainly there will be similar life cycle for each of its components. Suppose one of the components doesn't even fall anywhere near the life cycle estimation and fails much earlier than anticipated or it deteriorates much faster; we call it "accelerated deterioration". Then we must first identify, analyse and put solution in place to make it run at reasonable rate and state. This we call as repair or maybe be inspect and repair stage.

Now, the second type is that it's not failing fast, but it's not a reasonable life of the spare. For example, we knew that the bearing should run around 8000 hrs and fails at 5000 hrs. Then, something must be wrong. What we do to bring it back to a reasonable life, say around 7000 hrs or more, is called corrective maintenance.

Time-based maintenance is predominantly employed where we know that the life of the spare part or the subcomponent is reasonably stable. That means, in the example of bearing, if we can get around 7000 hrs of life consistently, even though slightly less than what OEM recommends, it gives us assurance that we can know in advance that failure is due in some hrs. accordingly we can plan and respond to the preventive part of the maintenance. This is how time-based maintenance works.

"And what about condition-based maintenance?" asked the old man.

"As the name suggests, it is condition-based; we check the condition and then decide the maintenance action plan-simple." Replied Rakesh.

"So you check the condition of the subcomponent by stopping the machine and then doing the inspection, evaluate and then take action, so how is this different that inspection and repair?" asked old man.

"When we day condition based, then we assume that there are some indicators which give us the condition of the status of condition of the part, in real time. If we don't have that, then there is no meaning of condition-based. This is more applicable with newer machines where the condition-based measurements are available for critical parts of the machine. Sometimes, as part of the improvement in the process, our team can do some methodology to know the condition of the part beforehand. Some temperature sensors, movement sensors, vibration sensors, etc., give real-time online data, based on which we can take a call for maintenance. The benefit of this type of maintenance is that we get a response time, during which we can arrange material, man and method to do the work. And ask a planned shut of machine." Explained Rakesh

"That's nice"

"but the downside is that not every critical parameter can be captured because the cost of capturing that data can be prohibitively costly. The ROI thing doesn't work out. Similarly, in time based maintenance, we can have error of our judgement, sometimes we face an early failure or sometimes the part is not required to be changed, but when we open the machine, it is prudent to change it, as it saves unplanned need for change of same part at later date. So we lose the cost due to unused life of spare." Rakesh replied.

"Ultimately, it is about striking a balance between both approaches", continued Rakesh.

"Wonderful," said the old man. "Amazing, you are quite knowledgeable about this topic, huh!"

"I don't know how much, but I know few things, but the things that you explained till now, I wish I knew it earlier. I read some articles and books on maintenance, everyone tells what should be done, but no one tells me "How". I think, with the discussions that we had today, I can derive a 'how" part myself," Replied Rakesh.

"What about overhaul thing?" asked the old man.

"It all depends on what company prefers based on cost and time factors, e.g. there is a process industry, and the equipment more or less run for a fixed time of year, regularly. It could be a planned way of running, or it could be based on the business cycle in the year. But in any case, the company gets around 15 to 20 days of shutdown, then it's worth keeping equipment running the rest of the time and planning a detailed overhaul for critical equipment. Another example could be a company where there are boilers. This is the equipment that you cannot shut down or start at will and whim, and the startup and shutdown costs are very high. Then, the planned shutdown period of the rest of the plant is taken in parallel with this equipment overhaul time. It saves time for everyone as well as another process. The only condition is that the equipment should run continuously between two overhaul periods. If that is possible, then overhaul is the best option.

All the time-based and condition-based maintenance is not at all in the picture. This requires meticulous resource planning and focussed skill sets." Explained Rakesh.

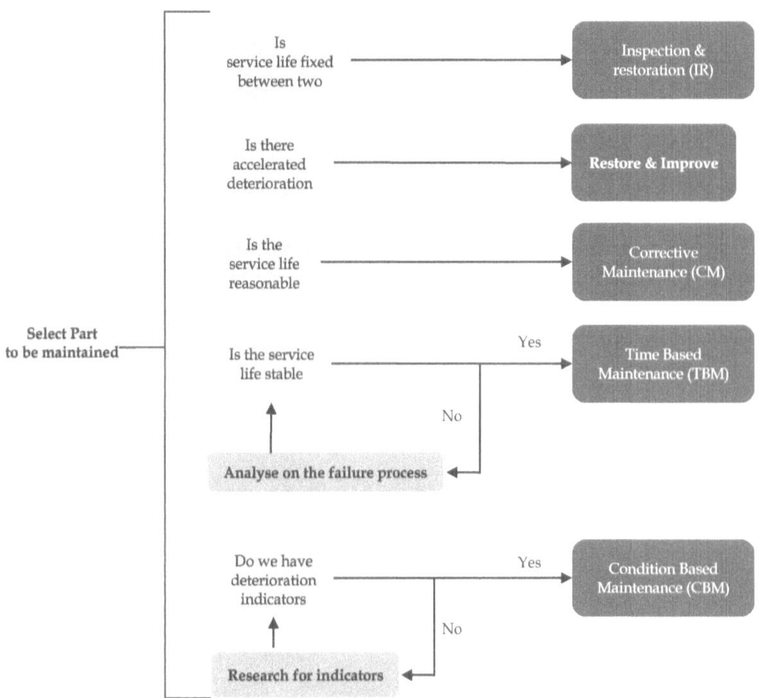

"Superb, so many things I learnt from you today," the old man said joyfully.

"What next? I told you what types of maintenance are; what did you have in mind?" asked Rakesh.

"If you recollect, we had virtually broken down the machine to the last level, where the subcomponent of the equipment was taken for maintenance purposes. The types of maintenance you told me have to be applied to each of that subcomponent or spare. The logic of assigning that to the part is already known to you. You just now explained it to me. So it should not be difficult."

"Isn't it too time-consuming?" Rakesh expressed with narrowing of his eyes.

The old man looked at him in despair, "Again? It's the same thing we discussed, no? This is to be done once for each type; the rest is only copy and paste to other equipment, 80% of the time. Oh! God!. Do I start all over again?"

"No, no, don't worry, I was just kidding, yeah, it is understood", smiled Rakesh when replying.

The old man looked at the watch, there was still about 3 hour to dinner time, train was running late, said "lets discuss further, we still have lot of time before dinner is served."

He continued, "Once you put the type of maintenance in the next column of the equipment sheet, you will find that you can club the types of maintenance together for better understanding."

S.no	Machine	Assembly	Sub-Assembly	Component	Sub-component	Maintenance Method
1	Computerised Numeric Control machine	Automatic Tool Changer	Tool magazine (tool storage side)	Tool pockets	Tool lock	TBM
2					Tool lock spring	CBM
3				Driven Sprocket	Sprocket	IR
4					Drive chain	CM
5					Sprocket bearing	TBM
6					Shaft	CBM
7				Hydraulic motor	End connectors	IR
8					Motor seals	TBM
9					Hydraulic hoses	TBM
10				Positioning sensors	Proximity sensor	IR
11					Sensor connector	IR
12				Tool unlock cylinder	End connectors	IR
13					Piston seals	TBM
14					Hoses	TBM

"For "Inspect & repair" & "Corrective Maintenance", once it's done satisfactorily, these items would move to either overhaul (OH), time based maintenance (TBM) or condition based maintenance (CBM). So this sheet is a kind of dynamic sheet, and it will change in a review mechanism every six months till every item falls under either TBM, CBM or OH. Once you group types of maintenance, you are very clear about how things are to be planned. I am not sure, but if I guess it correctly.

1. CBM thing will either have alarm systems or an operator checklist for monitoring only. As soon as something is found in the area of response, you would plan it out and club the action with the next planned shutdown for Time-based maintenance.

2. TBM, anyway, is clubbed together, and you plan it with your department teams

3. An overhaul is also a kind of TBM, but the spread is wide.

Am I correct in understanding?" asked the old man.

"Have you ever been wrong, Babuji?" laughed Rakesh.

The old man smiled back and continued, "Now you tell me, what is the next order of action?"

Rakesh mentally recapped the recent discussion.

1. We split the equipment into function and system

2. Then into assembly -subassembly-component -subcomponent

3. Then, I did the material planning with inventory levels

4. Before that, we assigned criticality to the last part that we maintain.

5.   Then, we decide what type of maintenance is to be done on each part

6.   Combine the parts for better planning methods

"Now what?" thought Rakesh. Immediately shouted, "Now what, nothing else, actual work to be done on the part. We have material, and we know when to maintain it and what to do. Do we do work?"

The old man gazed at him, "Will you start working directly? Or will you look or inspect the parts first? To know what is happening or what has happened?"

Rakesh felt embarrassed but laughed out, "Of course, first we observe, analyse and then do work"

"Great to know you are still in your senses", replied the old man and continued, "see, here comes the famous point of making checklist. Once you take a shutdown of a machine for either TBM or CBM, what things are you going to check?. This you must be doing it anyway, right?"

"Yes, this we already do"

"Nice, but do you directly jump to work, or do you inspect and then do the work? What process do you follow?" asked the old man.

"Once the checklist is there about what to do, what is there to follow more, we start the work." Replied Rakesh with a frustrated tone.

"Hmm, tell me, how many times has it happened that you completed the TBM or CBM on maintenance shutdown, handed over the machine for production, and the next day or within one or two days, the machine is under breakdown again?"

"Many times"

"And why is that?"

"People who are doing work, they are not attentive while doing their work, or sometimes the time is insufficient, so they just box up the machine back with some unfinished work as it is. People mistake, what else can I say?" replied Rakesh.

"Next time, follow the below principle of work; I will tell you more about it. First, write down some steps that you will ensure are followed every time the PM is done on any equipment.

1. Ensure that the "doer" has read the checklist.

2. He has understood each line item of the checklist.

3. All tools and tackles needed are with him/her

4. The most important thing now,

    a. Once he starts doing the checklist, a few things may need to be done under the power-on condition and a few things only after the power-off condition.

    b. In any case, ALL THE CHECKLIST POINTS MUST BE INSPECTED FIRST.

    c. Before starting any rectification work as per checklist points.

5. Once the inspection of all points is done, rectification starts ONLY after you.

    a. Prioritise work based on Safety, Quality & time taken to rectify the discrepancy found during inspection.

    b. If the "doer" is not capable or authority to decide this, superiors should do this to help him.

This small change in process will help you a lot."

"I can understand prioritisation helps, but what impact will it have for work in hand?" asked Rakesh.

"Assume that your "Doer" has 20-point checklist. He starts working on a checklist based on power on/off conditions and starts the inspection. On 3rd point, he finds abnormality and immediately starts taking action. Imagine you have taken a shutdown for 4 hrs, and this 3rd point itself is going to take 2 hrs to rectify. What happens to other work on the same checklist?. Are you able to imagine?" asked the old man & continued " out of the balance 17 points, some may be more important, relevant to immediately functioning of machine, some of them may cost you more if still run under bad condition, worst case may be of any unsafe thing left attended may cause accident. These all will be unattended, unnoticed till the machine is available next or if it comes under unplanned breakdown. During that time, you would be under pressure to restore the machine. The quality of maintenance work may suffer while working during breakdown conditions. I am not saying it will happen, but we know that quality suffers when working under stress. So, all things can be avoided if we first inspect and cover all points; then you will see that out of 20 points, only 10 require attention. Guage the time taken for rectifying all during this shut down or you need to extend shutdown or you can do adjustment so that it runs with acceptable performance till you get to it in next planned maintenance time."

"Nobody wants to extend the shutdown time", Rakesh quickly replied

"Ha! Ha! Whoever denies you, ask him this question: Can you afford 2 hrs of extra extended shutdown OR 6 hrs of unplanned downtime, that too during night time?, I am sure you will get all the support you need. But you have to be true to yourself. Don't fall back for help on "created" situations. It has following benefits for sure

1. After inspecting all 20 points, you know the status of each point. Thereby bringing confidence to your team that things will run till we get to the next planned shutdown.

2.	Sometimes, you cannot finish all the points because your team member resources are not in the required numbers.

3.	Sometimes, several people are there, but the skilled member is absent

4.	Sometimes, you depended on correct material, but the material is not fitting now.

5.	Sometimes, due to production pressures, you will have to shorten your shutdown time.

Under all these cases, or any other case, you will at the least be sure of what all is pending on the list and how many run hrs can be expected from the machine before you get a machine for maintenance. This confidence with data from the checklist is good enough for you to plan out your next maintenance time in a better way. And even after doing all these, you still feel that something unsafe is still operating or something that will affect the quality of the product. You can communicate to all the people and processes that are going to get impacted, including your superiors. That way, the communication is improved, and if anything does go wrong, it's a collective and shared responsibility of all those people who were part of the decision making. It could be a collective calculated risk."

"Lovely, it is a wonderful tool to implement, I mean process", said Rakesh enthusiastically.

"See, a small, thoughtful and organised way of working can go a long way in life. And mind you, it is not just professional life; your personal life will also be better if you understand this." Replied the old man.

HOW DO WE DO, WHAT WE DO

Practice makes a man perfect.

Meanwhile, the tea vendor was just passing by, and the old man shouted and called him back. The old man asked Rakesh if he would have another round of tea. Rakesh agreed.

This time, the old man paid for both of them. They enjoyed the tea, looked out of the window and chatted about the weather and the monsoon season in that area and region.

Both finished the tea, disposed the cups in the waste bag and settled back again for further discussion. Rakesh was looking at Oldman inquisitively, wondering what was going to come out of his mouth next.

The old man sensed this and said, "Yes, yes, now we move to 3rd M, that is method."

"Phew! Thank god, finally moved to the next M," exclaimed Rakesh.

"Why, you did not like what we talked about process of TBM, CBM etc, it's really important. you see?"

"I was just excited to go to the next step, not that I did not like what you taught me," replied Rakesh.

"Now that we know what to do, where to do, why to do, now we move to understand 'how' to do. And that is called Method." Said the old man.

"You know how to do maintenance?" Rakesh asked, surprised.

"No, I don't know about how to do maintenance, but I can help you create a system to support maintenance by answering the 'How" part of it." Nailed the old man.

"You have a machine part or subcomponent where you know what to do; you need to just write down HOW you do what you do. In a step-by-step procedure, again, ask relevant questions from the 5W-1H method on this written script. This script is called Standard Operating Procedure (SOP) in the rest of the systems, but for maintenance, we can call it STANDARD MAINTENANCE PROCEDURES – SMP. Thus, for each part, you write the SMP for repair or replacement." Said the old man.

"Again, before you start cribbing about "lot of work", these SMPs are written only once but applicable to every equipment that will have this as their subcomponent. Effectively, you will have to work only 40% and you get 100% benefit. Plus, even if you change jobs or companies, this SMP is with you lifelong. Imagine the kind of benefits that you get out of doing one thing correctly."

"Yes, Babuji, no more complaints. I understand your point completely. We did make some SOPs for our work, but they were not complete & also not of good quality. It was more for the tick in the box for audit purposes. But this time, I will do something different and will take all the team members together to do this, distribute the work and see how much we can do. We can distribute the goals over 2 or 3 years, not that everything is done in this year itself."

"Fantastic, now you are getting my point. Organise, communicate, distribute, follow-up and review. Start with A ranking equipment for this year, and do the B ranking equipment next year. C ranking equipment will have a different strategy for maintenance altogether.

S.no	Machine	Assembly	Sub-Assembly	Component	Sub-component	Maint. Method	Criticality Ranking	Maint. Procedure
1	CNC	ATC	Tool magazine	Tool pockets	Tool lock	TBM	B	SMP-1
2					Tool lock spring	CBM	A	SMP-2
3				Driven Sprocket	Sprocket	IR	B	SMP-3
4					Drive chain	CM	C	SMP-4
5					Sprocket bearing	TBM	B	SMP-5
6					Shaft	CBM	A	SMP-6
7				Hydraulic motor	End connectors	IR	C	SMP-7
8					Motor seals	TBM	A	
9					Hydraulic hoses	TBM	C	
10				Positioning sensors	Proximity sensor	IR	C	
11					Sensor connector	IR	C	
12				Tool unlock cylinder	End connectors	IR	C	SMP-7
13					Piston seals	TBM	A	

Nice, good that you understood it very quickly. Saves my time as well. You are smart and intelligent, huh!" Replied the old man, praising Rakesh for the first time. The extended sheet may look like the image below when you write and update the SMP number against the subcomponent.

"See, SMP-7 is repeated for certain subcomponents, which means that you can write it once and use it multiple times." Explained the old man.

"Yes, that is correct, I got it"

"Simple, so that is what is Method part of the 4 M's. The only thing remaining is about how you write a meaningful and helpful SMP. I am sure you would be aware of writing SOP for the process, right? This is no different; some points are different, but the rest are similar. The fun is in writing it down and making it a habit to write down various SMPs whenever time permits or the need is there. The basic set of SMPs must be in place. Six monthly or yearly reviews can help amend it to various revisions. This will happen when our teams' knowledge levels start growing with this kind of SMP availability. "Said the old man.

"Another beautiful part of it is" continued the old man, "whenever there is change of person in department, like someone resigns, or new person joins, or if there is change of job role, you have this whole bunch of written down procedures that the new person can go through whenever he finds time and need. The knowledge repository is there. This drastically reduces the learning curve of the person. In addition to that, you can use this SMP as a base to evaluate people's skill levels as well. We will discuss this next."

"Can you tell me what all do you normally include in while making SOP?" asked the old man to Rakesh.

Rakesh drew the table and explained.

"Of course, these are guidelines, you can always choose to add or delete some points. Most important is that the 'doer' understands this before he starts the work." Continued Rakesh, while he tried to make this up in his diary and showed it to the old man.

STANDARD MAINTENANCE PROCEDURE

SMP-No.- 124 Date & Rev no.

SMP Description: Centrifugal water pump

1. Equipment Name: Water pump

2. Equipment Number:

3. Time required: 4 hrs

4. Manpower resource: 1 mechanical technician + 1 Helper

5. Material Required:

	Specification	Quantity
Mechanical Seal	Part no of manufacturer	1
Bearings	6205 / 6308	1 each
Gaskets	Part nos.	4
Oil Seals	50-40-5 mm	2
Lubrication Oil	SAE 40	2 L
Impeller nut	Specification, Left hand thread	1
Shaft Sleeve	Part no	1
Casing bolts	Half /Full thread, length	6
Gland plate bolts	Size, length	2

6. Tools required:

    a. Ring type spanners, Flat spanners, Allen Keys – Sizes & qty, hammer, chisel, circlip pliers, etc

7. Do's & Don'ts

Do's	Don'ts
Get permit to work	Take more than required people with you
Power off, check and confirm	Bypass the power / energy source
Clean area before and after doing maintenance	Lift heavy weight unnecessarily
Dispose all the used material appropriately	Open the seal without isolating the valves
Appropriate PPE	

8. Disassembly: Follow the disassembly procedure as per the OEM Maintenance Manual *(cross reference of that SMP can be mentioned here)*

9. Repair / Replacement: Follow the Seal replacement / Gland replacement/bearing replacement SMP

10. Assembly: Follow Assembly procedure and confirm by doing measurements to confirm that assembly is correct. *(cross reference of that SMP can be mentioned here)*

11. Trial and testing: Follow the trial, inspection & testing SMP.

12. Close the work order and update the record in the log book.

"Nice, wonderful, good to go." Appreciated the old man.

"So method is not a lengthy topic, if you have context and understanding of previous things that we learnt before coming to method. Do you think our flow of thoughts and understanding are moving in the correct direction?" asked the old man.

"Very much. I am thrilled to understand and learn this"

"The next thing we will understand is the last M, Man in the 4 M's," the old man said while straightening up his back and stretching his body.

THE MAN

Creator, the reason

"Till now, we have discussed and understood about Machine, Material, Method and now we embark to understand Man. This is important because Man is the one who is going to implement things and do the work. So, in our scenario, he knows the machine to work on, he has materials with him, and he has understood the method also. We now discuss about what are attributes of this Man, while he is expected to work. Let's understand it." Said the old man and continued.

"There are many categories or say attributes to the workforce that is employed in the factory, there are broad category of technical and non-technical, say non-technical would be like admin, HR, finance etc who may not be needed to be expert or knower of the technicalities of the product or the process of manufacturing. Hence, they are not professionals in the product field per se. We can look at it in a broad sense as"

Based on Profession	
Electrical	Mechanical
Electronics	Civil
Mechatronics	

Based on Experience & Exposure	
Equipment based exposure	Years based exposure

Based on Systems		
5S	Fire Fighting system	Safety systems
	Project Management	Capex management
	ERP	HR

So, people come from different backgrounds and experiences. But in the factory, they are expected to add value and deliver outcomes in one of the 3 ways that I just wrote for you.

1. People come with their specific education background to do something in their field of education.

2. Once they get experience, it is in two ways.

    a. Exposure/experience in terms of number of years, which is like a deeper learning in a singular field or equipment OR

    b. Exposure based, i.e. exposure to various equipment – similar or different but in different companies. For example, one person may have experience in air compressors for 10 years in one company. If he changes companies, he may be exposed to new make air compressor or different rating air compressor or different type of air compressor, but in principle the air compressor by its working and identity remains same. That is what I meant by exposure to equipment.

3. Lastly, there are some attributes due to the system working in any company, say, safety system, first aid, ERP, project management or Capex management, etc. These systems are more or less the same or similar in concept as well as implementation to a great extent in all the companies, so once you learn it in one company, it's all the same or almost the same.

With this awareness, we try to evaluate who is fit for which work or job. This can be applied to all the functions in the factory. That would need a tweak in the criterion for each function, but as we are focused on maintenance function only, let's stick to it for some more time." Concluded the old man.

"That is impressive. I never thought about this in such a manner. Separate, Categorise, analyse, and put them back together. Nice method. We used this to learn equipment functioning as well, right?" said Rakesh.

"Very much correct", replied the old man.

"There is a 4-quadrant approach to developing the skill of any person or employee, or for that matter, ourselves.

1. When we have only read about the subject and we are aware about it. This is called training, i.e. someone tells you what all things are there in the machine or equipment, how it operates, do's and don'ts, etc. You have not yet worked on it & it's more of theoretical knowledge.

2. The next level is when you work on it with your own hands and understanding but under someone's supervision. At this stage, you are free to work, but the decision-making at the critical point of deviation is still not your baby. Because you are not ready yet. The supervisor decides on your part, and then you start learning the decision-making process while you're working on a particular matter. This exchange of work, juncture of decision making, actual decision making and finally the result and its calibration with expectation, all happens in this stage.

3. The more often you do the work, the more experience increases and you are exposed to various conditions based on a variation of inputs, and thus, your decision-making improves. A condition comes where you have experienced almost 80% of variations, and you are fully equipped to take a decision. At this point, you no longer need supervision, & you can work independently.

4. The next stage is an expert level stage, where on the particular subject you have enough experience and exposure that you can start training other people and you become a trainer.

This may sound very easy as we sit and talk, but it takes enormous effort, patience, and focused practice and patience. These 4 levels are normally represented in 4 quadrants of a circle." Explained the old man while drawing the boxes in Rakesh's diary.

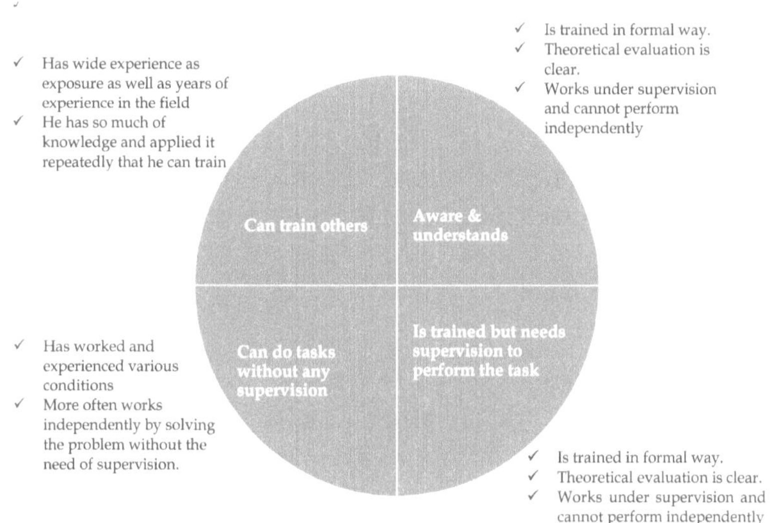

"This is what I was talking about. Put it up in a matrix or a quadrant, and it's easy to understand." Continued the old man.

"This is amazing, this will help us to evaluate anyone on a certain topic. I can evaluate myself first in this way and see where I stand in terms of management expectations for the promotion, etc. It's a very nice tool. Thank you." Rakesh expressed himself.

"But this is just a start, the crux is how do you map this theme or logic to evaluate your people on skill levels?" old man expressed.

"How? For people with a professional background, it's easy to evaluate by giving them a simple test and seeing where they stand," replied Rakesh hurriedly.

"That's good, and what about the experienced ones? Do you want to test them on their college syllabus or curriculum after 10 years of service? Huh!?. They will beat you up." Replied old man laughingly.

"This is where your SOPs and SMPs come into picture, and that is why it is to be understood at the last of the 4 M's. See, you have SOP and SMP for each of your work. Maintenance work, machine work or what not, right? Apply these 4 quadrants approach and see for yourselves, which one of your supervisor or staff belongs to which quadrant? Simple," old man explained and threw his hands in the air, "you don't need anything else; you have developed everything before you reach this stage. Try it out on one of your known persons right now and see."

Rakesh thought of someone and, at the same time, thought of one of the works that he already had a simple SMP. He was surprised to understand that even though he was working with them for 6 years, out of 6 staff people, only 2 could be thought of working in the 2nd quadrant, forget about the 3rd quadrant. Rakesh was smiling inside, and old man could comprehend that he had found something simple and amusing.

"What is it?" asked the old man.

"Nothing, this is such a simple tool, but very effective. I tried to map all my 6 staff supervisors on a simple SMP, which they were doing before I joined, but when I see objectively, they will not be cross the second quadrant." Replied Rakesh.

"And that's precisely the problem, my son. Now you get it? Your experienced staff people are not able to "work without supervision" i.e. 3rd quadrant. Even after so much experience, what is the fun in working then?. Now you know where to put efforts, which people can be easily shifted to 3rd quadrant by giving proper exposure and experience. Then, they are ready to take your load of work. Then you will not find yourselves sandwiched between work, management and life. Isn't it true?" the old man enthusiastically explains as if he had found the key to the treasure.

The old man continued," Even though the evaluation of skill of any person becomes subjective, no matter how hard we try, but this process takes cares and remains objective to at least 80% of the time. Secondly, while we do evaluations, the employee also feels that there are mechanisms for evaluations and not just a tick in the box. There is more transparency in the system, and people feel that there are no "favour games" being played in the department and functions. Additionally, most importantly, people themselves know which area they have to improve upon. They don't just get a blanket statement like "improve your attitude, improve your tech skills", etc. Those are statements that do not tell exactly what the person is expected to work on and improve. Do you get me?. One single process takes care of many things and drastically reduces the team conflicts within no time. Yes, no system is perfect, and we can improve upon it over time. At the same time, people will also come about the limitations of any system. This makes a big change in attitude towards work."

Rakesh had no words to say, he was more serious than a few minutes before. Just looked out of window few times and then looked at the diary and then the old man.

Took his hand towards the old man, shook his hand in gratitude, and thanked him. He looked like a drained man. He now wanted a cigarette and nothing less. If left to him, he might have smoked two cigarettes in succession. He told the old man that he needed to smoke before anything else.

"But we are not finished yet. We will finish in another hour and will go for a smoke together." Told the old man.

But Rakesh was in no mood to listen to him. he got up, straightened his trousers, looked for a cigarette packet and lighter and asked the old man, "All that thing later on; now I need a smoke. I will look at rest of things after that".

After 15 to 20 minutes, both came back and settled at their seats. The old man got freshened up in the meantime, while Rakesh was still smoking.

"So what more remains? I think there is another half an hour for dinner," said Rakesh.

"Yes, maybe. Let's finish what we have in hand. So, we finished the 4-quadrant approach for the skill level of people. Use this for the technician level also. It will give wonderful results. But don't forget to evaluate them against professional background as you said as well as SMPs both. You can expand it by creating levels based on the years of experience and time required to learn all those skills. Let me give you some examples. That will make it clearer.

Sr. No	Levels of competency	Requirement of level	Skill Level (quadrant level)
	L1	Using measuring instruments like Vernier calliper & screw gauge etc	Q3
		Fits and tolerances	Q3
		Fasteners like – nut and bolts, types, uses etc	Q2
		Tools and types, usage and upkeep	Q2
		Alignment, workshop practices, lathe, drill machine, grinding operations & maintenance	Q3
		Documentation & reporting (logbook, history cards, breakdown slips, next shift communication etc)	Q3
	L2	Reading hydraulic circuit diagram	Q2
		Reading Pneumatic circuit diagrams	Q3
		Sensors & types (Temp, pressure, proximity)	Q3
		Safety in the factory (preliminary & level 1 - mostly self)	Q3
		Documentation & reporting	Q4
		Troubleshooting and Analysis	Q2

"In this, if you see, there is professional knowledge required. More often the knowledge learnt but not used for long time get lost and in you don't repeat it, you lose it for ever. Here, the same thing happens; you evaluate them in each criterion and put them into Q1 to Q4. Then, you put in the next column, what quadrant do you wanted that person to be with his experience or job role requirement. The gap in this evaluation will tell you and the employee both the area of working on improving the skill levels. See, it's that simple. Another example could be that in the evaluation criterion, you put SMP numbers and evaluate them in terms of quadrants. Normally, you would want them to work in Q3, but not all will be there. So again, you come to know what needs to be done and on whom. In addition to this, the beauty of this is, if you could make out till now, you come to know about who all are in Q3 and Q4 in certain aspects. Those are people whom you can rely on and put to work first, before you get to solving the problems. You can use the Q4 person to train others, not necessary that you only have to become trainer for all. Thus, you can use this tool effectively in many more ways; the limit is decided by you and no one else. Even "permanent contractor" types of staff or workmen can also be evaluated using this. These kinds of people are always there in your department. We do not put them on our payroll due to purely commercial or long-term liability perspectives, but they are more or less part of our company by default. Happy?"

"Happy? It's a very small word, Babuji. I cannot thank you more; I don't know how to express my gratitude." Said Rakesh.

"No worries, do correct things in life and do well, that will be ok with me. few more thing before we close this discussion and learning and by the time dinner comes." Said the old man and continued. "The pending things for discussion are

1.   The scheduling of the work – when and how?

2.   The time cost of the maintenance.

Let's look at the scheduling of the maintenance work. May think that how come we are talking about this, doesn't seem to be the sequence of flow of thoughts that I talked about. To an extent, you are right; we could have discussed this when we talked about TBM and CBM, etc. At that time, we didn't know how much time any maintenance work would take. We had a checklist, we knew what to do, but 'how' to do was missing, so I thought we will work on Method part, and then we can bring back the topic for discussion again."

"Yeah, I also thought so because it's like we forgot something and now want to fill it up, but with you, it doesn't look like that you forgot it." Said Rakesh jokingly.

"I am not that good, but I can also forget. I am old now. But anyway, I was telling you about the how part of the work. In SMPs, you looked at how things will be done. And in the TBM/CBM case, you looked at what to do part, "When to do" will have to be looked in combined aspect." Explained the old man and continued further. The TBM has to be worked out with some frequency of checks, and CBM has to be on a condition-based basis. In both cases, you seek some time for maintenance. But how do you know how much time you will need to do maintenance?"

"Based on our experience, it's not that difficult,, said Rakesh.

"That's right, experience is one thing, and to back it up with data makes it more solid. I was trying to make you think about the SMP now. Each SMP has written down instructions for the work. Can this not become your repository data for the amount of time it takes to do the work? Not the first time, but if you keep a record of it and you do the same SMP 5 times, average out the time. That will be your estimated time to complete the maintenance task, isn't it? What you say?" asked the old man.

"From where do you think all such points, Babuji? You are lying to me; you are something else, and you tell me something else about yourself. I am 100% sure now. I have not met even the consultant they hired for our factory to explain things in such a superb way. Who are you? And what work do you do?" asked Rakesh in a mixed tone of voice of feeling wonderful and amazed and at the same time doubtful also.

"I am a retired old man with nothing to do, so I thought, why not help some frustrated being like you? If it has helped you, my work is done, and I am successful." Replied the old man.

"ok, you don't want to tell me, that's ok. What were you telling me about the maintenance time planning?"

"Yep, so from SMP, you get the approximate or estimated time required for work. Similarly, from the TBM / CBM chart, you get the frequency of work. Based on that, you can always project the next month's maintenance-related equipment shutdown hours required. You can always keep on calibrating these time limits. But you will have things to start with. It can be a revision "0", and then it can go on to R1, R2 kind of revisions." The old man said. If you look at it, it will look like this. There, you can find the time required for Weekly work, Monthly work, or yearly work, etc., so the number of hours of non-availability of the machine can be communicated to the production department well in advance for their capacity planning purpose. Of course, this will not happen overnight, it will take some months. For Critical category machines, you can target first and then the B ranking equipment. Don't go by the figures that I have put here, they may not be correct. You will have to figure out what that time will be by repetition and averaging out the time taken.

S.no	Sub-component	Maintenance Method	Freq of maintenance	Maintenance Procedure	Time Required (hrs)
1	Tool lock	TBM	W	SMP-1	6
2	Sprocket bearing	TBM	W	SMP-5	0.5
3	Motor seals	TBM	Q		6
4	Hydraulic hoses	TBM	W		2
5	Hydraulic hoses	TBM	W		2
6	Piston seals	TBM	W		3
7	Hoses	TBM	M		2
8	Tool lock spring	CBM	D	SMP-2	6
9	Shaft	CBM	D	SMP-6	1
10	Drive chain	CM	Q	SMP-4	0.5
11	Sprocket	IR	M	SMP-3	1
12	End connectors	IR	M	SMP-7	0.25
13	Proximity sensor	IR	D		1
14	Sensor connector	IR	M		0.25
15	End connectors	IR	Q	SMP-7	0.5

The above is for the time required for maintenance work. The same SMP also gives details of the manpower and the skill level required for the work. So, on similar lines, can we think of a similar table giving details of manpower resources? How will that look?" quizzed the old man.

This doesn't explicitly mention the skill level, but you can always populate this table. Remember, "these are guidelines"; you are free to add, modify, or delete whatever you want. But remember, the effort should be meaningful. It should not happen that people are collecting only data and have no time for analysis. Don't overdo anything."

"Are we together on this? Understood till now?" asked the old man again.

"Yes, yes, very much, no worry."

So the last thing that remains now is the "time cost of the maintenance".

S.no	Sub-Component	Check to be done	Standard	Actual	Category	Who can do it	Time Required (hrs)
1	Tool lock	Check lubrication level & top up if required	Half of sight glass		Mechanical	Machine Operator	0.25
2	Sprocket bearing	Bearing vibration	<1 mm/s2		Mechanical	Maintenance Technician	0.5
3	Hydraulic hoses	Tighten, if loose			Mechanical	Maintenance Technician	2
4	Hydraulic hoses	Replacement if leak or cracked			Mechanical	Maintenance Technician	2
5	Piston seals	Replacement			Mechanical	Maintenance Technician	3
6	Valve electrical connectors	Check 24 V supp-y & LED indicator			Electrical	Maintenance Technician	2
7	Sprocket	Check teeth condition			Mechanical	Maintenance Technician	1
8	Sensor connectors	Check for looseness and tighten, if loose			Electrical	Machine Operator	0.25

THE MEASUREMENT

How did we performed

"Before we enter into a discussion of time cost of maintenance, let's understand how do we measure our performance, that will give some insights about how to measure costs associated with maintenance work," the old man said.

"How do you currently measure the performance of the maintenance function? You must be already doing it?" asked old man.

"Yes, we measure the equipment-wise downtime and its % for the month. We also have month-on-month data for analysis. Management insists on these two items only; there are other measurements that I have heard like Mean time to repair (MTTR) and Mean time between failure (MTBF), and some say OEE is the best measurement for equipment performance. Never tried to get into those, didn't had time to finish daily work, where to find the time to get into these aspects?" said Rakesh and continued " now, with whatever you told me or taught me, I may find some time for my own to understand and implement it, whether management wants or not, it's a different matter."

"Correct. Do it for yourself first."

"Can you help me understand all the terms that you used just now about performance? OEE, I think, is Overall equipment efficiency. OEE) If I am correct?" asked the old man.

"It is overall equipment effectiveness and not efficiency. And it is equipment performance, not just maintenance performance." Replied Rakesh.

"Right, effectiveness and efficiency are two different things", mumbled the old man.

"Yeah, people say it is different, but I did not understand, if I don't want to measure it, why to unnecessarily load my mind with that effort?" laughed Rakesh.

"Efficiency is measure of how much correct are you doing, whatever you are doing. What you are doing is not necessarily correct or useful in a certain context. It is measured by how correct you are doing & not whether you are doing the correct thing for a certain context," the old man continued, "and effectiveness is like, first you have to ascertain the correctness of direction of work, how correct are you in choosing the direction of the work."

"Maybe the below table will help you understand and help you keep it memorised for a longer time. It is very important to understand the difference," said the old man.

"For example, if you want to travel from point A to point B, you can choose any process, how fast you reached there, if that is the measurement criterion, then estimated time vs actual time, is you efficiency. If it was fuel consumption that was measured, then plan vs actual consumption would be efficiency. In effectiveness case, if you reached correct destination will matter first, then the efficiency will be or should be looked at. The table below shows exactly that. Please understand this," said the old man while handing the diary back to Rakesh.

Doing Right things	Effective	Right Goals Achieved but not efficiently	Right Goals achieved & efficiently
	Ineffective	Wrong Goals & not achieved efficiently	Wrong Goals achieved efficiently
		Inefficient	Efficient
		Doing things right	

"Hmm, I can understand this. This is useful and easy to remember. So the OEE is effectiveness and not efficiency." Replied Rakesh.

"Ok, let me explain to you the measurements that we do and the other terms like MTTR and MTBF. We note the breakdown time and its frequency of occurrence at the very basic. You would know it. The difference between the start of breakdown and the end of breakdown is the downtime. & how many times it happens in a month-is the frequence of failure." Explained Rakesh.

"Now I will try to explain the MTTR first, with an example," and he started drawing something in his diary.

Assume that any particular equipment broke down in January and below was the downtime for 4 different occasions.

Total breakdown time for the period = (35+65+105+180)

= 385 mins

Number of times the equipment broke down   = 04.

Therefore, the Mean Time To Repair = (385/4)   = 96.25 mins.

So, the formula would be MTTR = (total time of breakdown/Number of Breakdowns).

It's generally expressed in minutes.

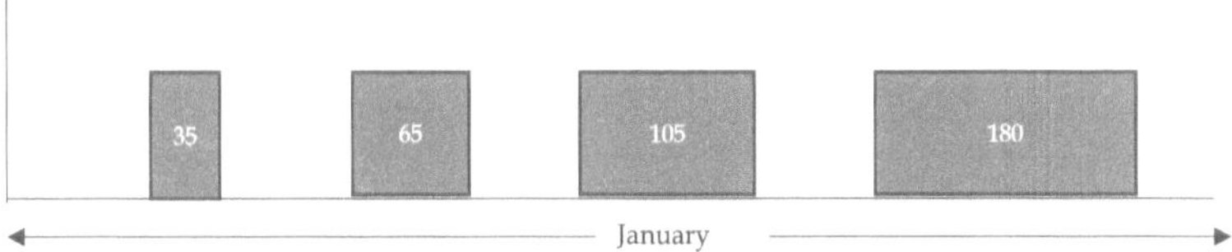

The same thing can be represented on the "mean" calculation for understanding as,

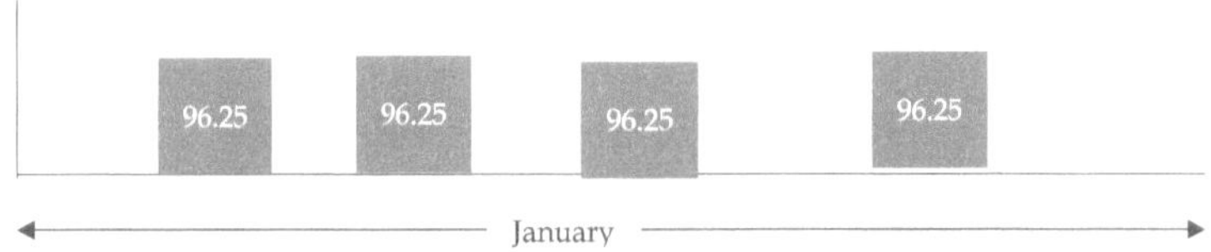

So, in the "mean time to repair" sense, the equipment, when it breaks down, remains under breakdown for 96.25 mins. Every breakdown reason may be different, but the MTTF doesn't take into account those details.

"Is this understandable, or am I too fast to explain?" asked Rakesh.

"No, no, perfectly fine, I understood this. I was in touch with my maintenance guy and heard these terms, but never went into details. Nice to know it now," replied the old man.

"So, next, I tell you about MTBF. I will keep the same example so that things can continue in the same flow for understanding the calculation and difference. With the same data of breakdown and assuming that a full month was available for production, this is for simplicity only; actually, you may have holidays, weekly days off and all that stuff. We can see data in different forms, as shown below.

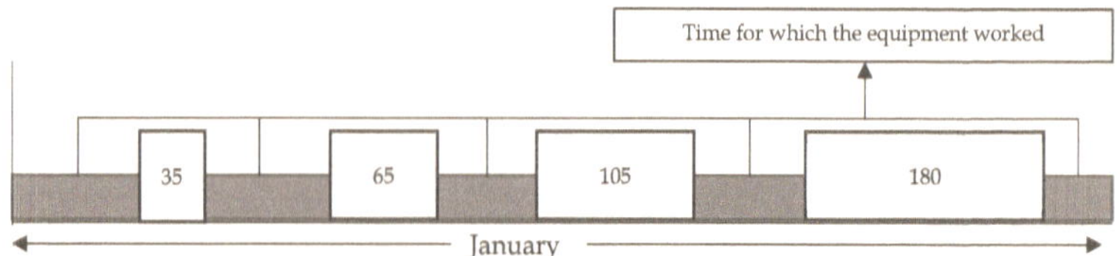

Started on the 1ˢᵗ of Jan and worked until 5ᵗʰ Jan and was under breakdown for 35 mins. Broke down on 11ᵗʰ Jan for 65 mins and

on 19ᵗʰ Jan for another 105 mins.

& lastly on 29ᵗʰ Jan broke down for 180 mins.

Total breakdown time for the period = (35+65+105+180)= 385 mins = 6.41 hrs

Number of times the equipment broke down = 04.

Total number of hours that machine could have worked in January =31*24 = 744 hrs.

Theoretically machine worked for = 744 – 6.41 = 737.6 hrs

Therefore, the Mean Time Between Failure = 737.6/04 = **184.4 hrs.**

So, the formula would be MTBF = (total time - total time of breakdown)/(Number of Breakdowns).

It's generally expressed in hours.

Again, if I represent it to what it means on the physical machine front, then

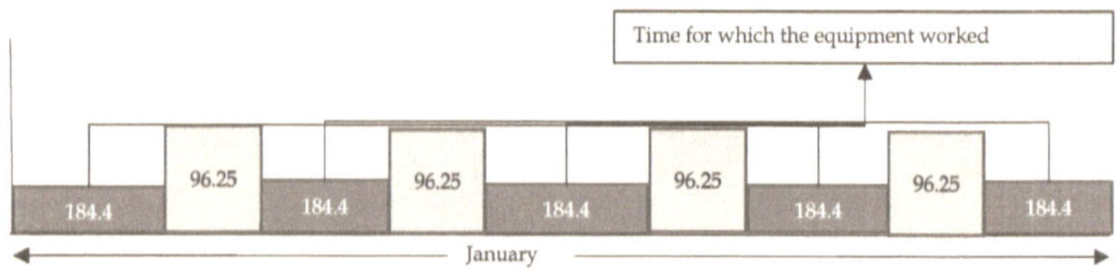

"It means the machine would run for 184.4 hours continuously and then have breakdown which lasts for 96.25 hrs. This is in the "mean" terms. Actually, on individual breakdown front, we may experience different durations of breakdown." Explained Rakesh.

"Hmm, not things are getting clear on these measurement terms. You measure this to understand and bring an improvement in it, right? So how do you relate this, or what do you do to reduce the MTTR and increase the MTBF? That is what our ultimate aim is." Asked Oldman enthusiastically.

"Kya Babuji, kidding me? Whatever you told me for so long and full day today, we have to do some improvement on man, machine, method, material and planning to improve this. What else?" Said Rakesh.

"If I am correct, the actionable point is for MTTR and not for MTBF. MTBF is a calculated term, therefore, you practically work to reduce MTTR, and MTBF will automatically get improved."

"Yeah, looks like, yes. Very much, I had not seen it in that way." Said Rakesh, looking at the diary and the formula that he wrote.

"That means – if the machine is down anyway and available for repair, then out of the remaining 3 M's, if you have material in hand, the MTTR is completely function of the Man Skill and for that you have SMPs in place. Right? So the focus should be on Skill development and material availability, in short." Concluded the old man.

Rakesh laughed, "Yeah, it is that easy, no worry at all, we can all go home and sleep well at night, Ha! Ha!."

Lastly, it is OEE, overall equipment effectiveness,

"Before we proceed to overall equipment effectiveness, we should talk about six big losses.

Generally, when we see analogy, we see six big losses as hidden losses. The best analogy is the iceberg. We all know what an iceberg is, and iceberg represents most of the time hidden items. When we look at the surface, we can visualize very small things, very small parts of the whole thing. But under the water, there is a big chunk that is invisible, and we do not work on those items. The six peak losses are hidden.

1.   Breakdown loss

2.   Setup and changeover loss

3.   Reduced speed

4.   Minor stoppages

5.   Rework and

6.   Scrap

Now, these six peak losses are connected to overall equipment effectiveness in a certain way.

Overall Equipment Effectiveness =

availability factor X **performance factor** X **quality factor.**

And what are these factors? Let us understand that.

The availability factor has two losses out of the six peak losses, which is

1.   breakdown loss and

2.   setup and change loss.

This means the machine or the equipment was not available for production.

During those times when setup was going on or changeover was going on or the machine was under breakdown. So the machine was not at all available to run.

Now, look at the performance factor, --

1.   Reduce speed and

2.   Minor stoppages.

If we say the availability factor, the machine is not available to run. But in the performance factor, the machine is available to run, but it is not running at the required speed. For example, the machine was to produce, say, 600 bottles a minute, but it is producing 500 bottles per minute because at high speed, the machine is making noise, so the operator has reduced the speed. So, the output is correct, but it is at a reduced speed.

Minor stoppages,

The definition of minor stoppages is anything equal to 5 minutes or less, which the operator cannot write down or cannot remember to write, or the amount of effort and time spent in writing that down is not worth it. Those are minor stoppages. But those minor stoppages, when cumulated, can have a bigger impact. To solve those minor stoppage problems, we have different techniques that we can take into a different topic.

Therefore, under the performance factor, these are the two portions of six losses, that are, reduced speed and minus stops.

Another analogy of performance would be an employee coming to the factory but having a headache or not feeling well. So on that day he is available in the factory but his performance is not up to the mark.

Lastly, the quality factor is a function of rework and scrap.

These are the two things that affect the quality. The quality factor is how you are producing the product the first time right.

Availability factor: The machine is not available to run.

In the Performance factor, the machine is available to run but is running at a reduced speed.

In the quality factor, despite running at a reduced speed, the output from the machine

has not been 100% first-time right.

A few things have gone into rework, and a few things have been scrapped. The net output is much less than the expectation or the design parameters. This is the overall equipment effectiveness." Rakesh concluded with taking a deep breath.

"Superb, so you knew what is first time right, and you were asking me about it." Joked the old man. "Seriously, you know a good amount of things about OEE, and that's good. Can you give any examples? For me understand correctly?"

OEE is calculated with one example.

Availability factor=(available time - breakdown time) / available time

Performance factor =

(actual number of items produced) /(numbers possible in runtime).

This runtime = (available time – breakdown - change over time - change over setup time).

The numerator of the availability factor would be the denominator in the performance factor for the number of items produced in the given time.

Quality factor,

Quality factor = (right first-time numbers produced)/ actual numbers produced.

This actual number produced is now the numerator in the performance factor now works into the denominator of the quality factor and that is the formula for calculation of overall equipment effectiveness."

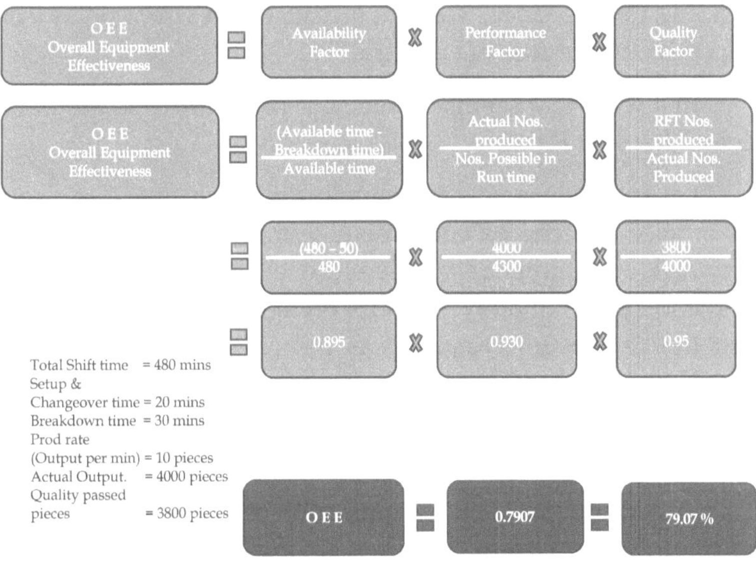

Rakesh explained this in his diary. The old man was satisfied and happy.

"So tell me now, you know what is the breakdown loss time, MTTR, MTBF, OEE etc, these are the time lost, and in business the lost time is money lost. If I say that these are the time costs of the breakdown, then what are the time costs of maintenance?" asked the old man and continued, "because that is where we started this discussion of measurement."

"I think the cost of maintenance about material cost is already discussed, what you want is time cost. Do you mean the time spent in doing maintenance is a cost?" asked Rakesh in surprise.

"Yes. Who wants maintenance? Nobody. At the same time, practically, it is unavoidable, for whatever reasons. Therefore, if not completely ZERO, people would want it to be as close as possible to ZERO. The time you spend in doing maintenance, say 6 hrs a week on every critical equipment (this is just an example, then the cost of these 6 hrs is the cost of doing maintenance. You can measure it in any way, as loss of production or loss of capacity."

"In a way, that seems correct, but practically, it cannot be Zero." Replied Rakesh.

"Let me trigger you for something interesting. Let's say, for a piece of complex equipment, you are spending 8 hours per week on maintenance. Therefore, every month, you have to spend approximately 32 hours on maintenance. Assuming that this is the time required as per all the SMPs that you use. Now, what will be your plan to reduce this time from 32 hours/month to, say, 30 hours/month?" Laughed the old man.

He continued, "This change will be your actual value addition to the system. I am not saying we have to make it ZERO every time, but the time you reduced on Planned maintenance is your actual value addition as maintenance department. This is much similar to the reduction in breakdown hours every month. If you can reduce 2 hrs on PM and 2 hrs on MTTR, then the improvement for the production of the factory will be (4 hrs/720 hours in a month) = 0.5% increase of production. That is a very big thing.

This is how you should look at things and decide upon the matrices for performance measurement."

"When you do this kind of analysis, you can also come up with a breakeven point or a point where all the things are balanced. Just to achieve a reduction in PM hours, you need a huge investment; then, it's better to stay with the existing plan. Everything must be looked at from a business perspective. I was only trying to explain the time cost of your maintenance work. You can have a different perspective and create a performance matrix around it, e.g. BD time / PM time or absolute PM time reduction. Manpower resources put in BD and PM and their cost, etc," concluded the old man.

Rakesh agreed and sighed, flipped a few pages from the diary and looked up to the old man. "This was a fantastic discussion and a time spent very usefully. I am glad that I met you. Thank you so much."

"I am glad too, it was worth spending time with you. I also learnt a lot. Young people are ambitious, and at the same time, they have a different view of the world. I get to see it when I talk to them. They are smart."

"With the material that you have noted down, do you think you can build a comprehensive system using these techniques? When you go back to same company or may be some other company?" asked the old man.

"Absolutely yes", he was about to say something more when the person serving the dinner interrupted.

Both took the dinner boxes and settled down by keeping them on a piece of newspaper.

Both of them washed their hands and came back to have dinner.

During dinner, they chatted about families, visiting each other's places if time permits, etc. Both of them finished the dinner.

"Did we discuss all topics that we started with?" asked the old man.

"Looks like nothing pending to me, but let me check. Nothing was missing in his diary," he nodded.

"I think, something you told me that it has changed over past 12 year, I am old and not in pace with the todays system, what was it? Environment and something" the old man was trying hard to remember it, suddenly he replied overjoyed, "yep, its compliance and environment son, see I remember."

"Yes, yes that's right, the matter of compliances and the environment related matters are now a day a serious thing. Statutory compliances are increasing day by day. How do we do work with so much of restrictions and limitations?" said Rakesh.

"Okay, I understand, but does anybody from management force you to do your job by overlooking these things? Such as statutory compliance or environmental compliance? I don't feel so, and if your boss asks you to deviate, then communicate well to him as well as the compliance committee, of course, seeing the trend of his behaviour. Maybe he is not up to the standard of understanding and needs a class in that himself. Even then, if it doesn't listen, you have a committee to report to. But that was on the people handling part. On the systems front, when we do the criticality assessment of the equipment, we just put one more item as Compliance; the environment is already considered in the safety aspect, if you recollect. That will solve your problem to some extent, and also you and your team would remember about it," the old man explained and continued, "what do you say? Will that help? The rest of the planning remains the same. Nothing changes. Few things would fall under TBM, and they will be taken care of as a routine. Nothing to worry about. Right?"

"Hmm, that can be the way out. On the systems front, these are taken care of, and at the same time, if it needs a deviation, we run to the boss or committee for deviation, etc. That was a good piece of advice. Nice. I will work on it like that." Replied Rakesh with confidence.

It was all heavy for Rakesh to discuss this for a long time. He desperately wanted to smoke.

Rakesh invited the old man for a smoke, but he declined, saying that he was too tired due to the long talks and wanted to go to bed early. Rakesh didn't force him and told him that if he needs any support during the night, the old man can call upon him.

Oldman was preparing his bed on the lower berth when Rakesh went for a smoke. He stayed there for about half an hour. Many thoughts were going through his head. Such a knowledgeable person, he thought, "I want to be like him, at least on professional front." Many thoughts crossed his mind about his colleagues, his work, his home, his PG. and suddenly he thought, "shit, I have not asked his name yet, I called him Babuji only". He rushed back to the seat and saw the old man was in a deep sleep.

He was sleeping like a child in a deep sleep. Rakesh didn't feel like disturbing him, looking at the way he was sleeping. "I will talk tomorrow morning and ask his name," he told himself and started preparing his bed.

In no time, he was also down in deep sleep, a full day occupied with interesting discussion that kept him charged, and when it came to sleep, he dozed off immediately.

THE LIFE - FULL OF SURPRISES

God closes one door to open another.

The next morning, when the tea vendor started shouting in the compartment, Rakesh woke up for tea. His berth was the top one, so he just bent down and looked for Babuji.

But Babuji was not there; the bedsheet, pillow, etc, were there, but Babuji was not there. He thought the old man must have gone to washroom to freshen up, so he laid back again and slept for another hour or so. The train took a halt at the station, now he woke up and climbed down. To his surprise, the old man was nowhere to be seen. He then asked the co-passengers if they have seen the old man. One of them said," That Babuji? he got down at the station at 3 am itself. He said that was his destination station."

Rakesh was shocked. "The old man spent time together full day, and without even telling me, he left the train. At least he could have said goodbye, I could have known his name." He sat down on berth and he was feeling very sad.

The train was late by around 4 hrs, and Rakesh reached his home. Met his parents and family members but did not discuss about what happened at the factory. He had spent around 5 days, when one of his friend from company called him and told him that the boss wants to speak to him and he should call back to office line.

Rakesh did not call back for a day and did not feel good about calling him. Nothing is going to change, so why unnecessary talk about the same topic?. Next day, he thought, let's hear what he has to say, what is harm in calling him up. He called his boss's office contact number. To his surprise, people at the factory were looking for him and wanted him to come back immediately. No reasons were discussed or told, the only thing shared was that the top management had mismanaged the whole incident and now it was to be rectified at earliest.

Rakesh had mixed feelings, he was not sure if he should be happy or still stay back and not join the company. He took one day to think it through. Then he spoke to his boss, took leave for another few days, stayed with family and then returned to the factory.

The day he went back to the factory, people were all around him, wanting to talk to him. Everyone wanted to explain what happened after he left and how things were discussed and talked about and how decisions were reversed by accepting mistakes, etc. All were happy that he was back in action.

After meeting all the people, he quietly went into his small cabin, opened the bag and took out his diary. Almost 20 days had gone by when he met Babuji, but it felt like he was sitting in front of him. One more thing that Rakesh felt bad about was that he could have checked Babuji's name with the ticket checker of the railways, but it did not strike him then. He got this idea when he left the railway station and started towards home in a bus. "How silly of me", he thought.

He opened the diary and started reading through the articles or matter that they both wrote in the diary on various topics. Rakesh was committed to converting these discussions into a full system. That will help him as well as the people around him.

He closed the diary and saw something there in the last pages of the diary. It was a small note.

"Son, it was nice spending time with you. God bless you. Remember that no matter what happens, your loyalty should be to your profession and not linked to any company or business. People will come and go. Your boss may change, but you cannot change yourselves as per the boss. Think about it, if there are three bosses in 3 years, each of different personality, which they would be, will you be able to change yourself for them. No way!. So you should be what you are, that is all. Always remember that "the evaluation of a decision making can only be done only when the decision is taken & implemented". Once the decision is taken and implemented, there is no way it can be undone. So do not beat yourself up, even if you commit a mistake. It is good quality in you that you are eager to learn, so keep that up. Whichever company you work for, be true to your intentions, own up to the responsibility of what you are doing, and build character. That is what people envy most. Hope I have been of some help to you. And if you think it was useful, you would also help someone in the same way or other.

One more strange thing came to my mind: whenever there is industrial unrest in any company, the first people who get beaten up are the HR fellows. Is it not an irony? The custodians of people get beaten up first, and the custodians of machines, i.e. maintenance people, are not even touched. Is it not surprising? A food for thought. I have not seen or heard about a maintenance guy getting beaten up by a unionised workforce, but if it happens, 1 in 10000, I am sure the guy deserved it. Ha!Ha!.

Goodbye and all the best, dear. Hope to see you again someday. By the way, there are some nice and pretty faces on the other side of the train compartment"

Rakesh could not stop laughing.

In the afternoon, around 4 pm, the reception desk called Rakesh and asked him to collect a parcel that had come in his name through the courier. Rakesh went there, looked at the parcel, and tried to see who had sent it. It just had the word "Babuji". Rakesh opened the parcel hurriedly and found a pack of cigarettes as gift wrap with a note.

"Sorry, could not do jugad on train, but I was sure that you will be called back to company, so sending it on the address. Do well and all the best."

Rakesh was surprised as to how this could come to the factory address. Spent a few days uneasy as this was not getting over. But after a month or so, with no luck to trace back who this "Babuji" was, he gave up.

Even though he moved on and could not find Babuji, he carried his treasure with him for his lifetime.

THOUGHTS

I shared the book with a few people for pre-reading and feedback. Some of them appreciated it and some of them were critical about a few things.

Why not include information about IoT and Industry 4.0?

The pure reason for sharing this set of knowledge is to help people understand the process of developing a system that can first sustain and then improve. The basic discipline in carrying out the work must be understood and implemented to its core. All other developments in technology are just built over this foundation.

Another concern was why not give readymade formats for implementation.

The reason lies in the way we think, if I give ready formats, the learner tends to stick to these formats only and hardly tries to improvise or think beyond what is written there. I wanted to leave some scope for the learner to be inquisitive and creative in designing his formats for his application and context. For more information, I have provided my contacts to get in touch with me.